Visitation Unimplor'd

Medieval and Renaissance Literary Studies

General Editor:
Albert C. Labriola

Advisory Editor:
Foster Provost

Editorial Board:
Judith H. Anderson
Diana Treviño Benet
Donald Cheney
Ann Baynes Coiro
Mary T. Crane
Patrick Cullen
A.C. Hamilton
Margaret P. Hannay
A. Kent Hieatt
William B. Hunter
Michael Lieb
Thomas P. Roche, Jr.
Mary Beth Rose
John M. Steadman
Humphrey Tonkin
Susanne Woods

Visitation Unimplor'd

Milton and the Authorship of *De Doctrina Christiana*

William B. Hunter

DUQUESNE UNIVERSITY PRESS
PITTSBURGH, PENNSYLVANIA

PR
3592
.R4
H84
1998

Copyright @ 1998 by Duquesne University Press
All Rights Reserved

No part of this book may be used or reproduced, in any manner whatsoever, without written permission, except in the case of short quotations for use in critical articles or reviews.

Published by

DUQUESNE UNIVERSITY PRESS
600 Forbes Avenue
Pittsburgh, PA 15282

Library of Congress Cataloging-in-Publication Data

Hunter, William Bridges. 1915–
    Visitation unimplor'd: Milton and the authorship of De Doctrina Christiana/William B. Hunter.
      p. cm. — (Medieval and Renaissance literary studies)
    Includes bibliographical references (p.) and index.
    ISBN 0-8207-0289-7 (cloth: alk. paper)
    1. Milton, John, 1608–1674—Religion. 2. Milton, John, 1608–1674. De doctrina Christiana. 3. Christianity and literature—England—History—17th century. 4. Christian literature, English—History and criticism. 5. Milton, John, 1608–1674—Authorship.
I. Title. II. Series.
PR3592.R4H84 1998
821'.4—DC21   98-10833
                                                                                CIP

CONTENTS

Introduction		1
1	Milton's Funeral and the Disposition of His Manuscripts	13
2	The Evidence of the Early Biographers	19
3	The Two Scribes	35
4	Canon and Treatise: Similarities and Differences	49
5	The Continental Context	71
6	Proof from Proof Texts	87
7	Divine Filiation	99
8	The Confounded Confusion of Chaos	121
9	Milton's Own Possible Testimony	135
10	Conclusions	149
Notes		159
Works Cited		177
Index		187

Tous ceux dont la vie se passe à chercher la vérité savent bien que les images qu'ils en saisent sont nécessairement fugitives. Elles brillent un instant pour faire place à des clartés nouvelles et toujours plus éblouissantes. Bien différente de celle de l'artiste, l'oeuvre du savant est fatalement provisoire. Il le sait et s'en réjouit, puisque la rapide vieillesse de ses livres est la preuve même du progrès de la science.—*Henri Pirenne.*

Introduction

Arthur Sewell wrote the first book entirely devoted to analysis of John Milton's works as they could be enlightened by comparison with *De Doctrina Christiana*, the religious treatise supposed by everyone to be his. Sewell was baffled by inconsistencies that he found between it and the canonic works. "The strange thing," he wrote, "is that the two poems and the play [*Paradise Lost, Paradise Regained* and *Samson Agonistes*] can only with difficulty be brought into relation with the treatise." As examples of such discontinuities he listed "the generation of the Son [of God] in time pursuant to a decree; the assumption by the Son, not only of human nature, but also of man," his death not only as man but as God, creation of the universe out of God's substance, and "reconciliation of man's free-will with God's foreknowledge." Sewell was perplexed: "Is it not strange? Here we have an intellect [Milton's] which has, whatever view we may accept of the date of *De Doctrina Christiana*, busied itself with the profound mysteries of the Christian religion. We turn to the poems... and we have to make subtle and unsatisfactory search for evidence of the conclusion of all this intellectual wrestling."[1]

As I and probably others have found, proving consistency between many of Milton's ideas and those

Introduction

expressed in the treatise can indeed be a "subtle and unsatisfactory search." All too often we have felt that we were forcing a lefthand foot into a righthand shoe. Recently, for instance, John Rumrich, in an analysis of Milton's views about chaos, has recognized that "*Paradise Lost* is not always consistent within itself, much less with *Christian Doctrine*,"[2] so that he can dismiss unargued differences of belief between poem and treatise. But such dismissal will not do: inconsistencies within the poem are not comparable with those between it and the treatise, and in no sense can the existence of the former conveniently excuse the latter. For example, the well-known conflict in the poem of the two locations of Hell—under foot or at the bottom of the universe—is a matter of geography, not dogma. The very existence of Hell, whatever its location, is a substantial Christian issue.

Some have thought that Milton was referring to a work of his own, one that he used to compose the treatise, when he entered in his *Commonplace Book* (a collection of quotations from his reading) 12 cross-references to a now-lost *Index Theologicus* that he and his amanuenses "probably had to hand" to assist them with *De Doctrina*, a record that would associate him directly with its composition.[3] But its known subjects, like "Of Church Property" or "Of Idolatry" are not those of the religious treatise we now have. It rather was a collection (like the *Commonplace Book* itself) of nonbiblical texts on religious topics. What would be very useful instead, had he been engaged with the treatise, would have been a collection of

Bible texts classified alphabetically by subject to support various dogmatic positions, which in a way *De Doctrina* illustrates and which finds a good parallel in Amandus Polanus's *Enchiridii Locorum Communium Theologicorum* (Basel, 1600). Many, perhaps most, of the biblical quotations in the treatise may derive from this compilation or a similar one. There is no evidence that Milton ever made one for himself.

As one especially concerned to understand his religious beliefs, I have often tried (more or less successfully) to bring canon and treatise into agreement. Only in the spring of 1991 did it occur to me (as apparently it had to no one since shortly after the publication of the treatise in 1825) that there was an alternative way out of these difficulties: the possibility that someone else wrote it. In favor of Milton's authorship, we can be sure that he was to at least some degree familiar with the work, for it appeared among his effects after his death. He shares with it many dogmas of the Reformed tradition. Furthermore, all the early biographers identified him as author of such a book, though they could not have seen the manuscript and could report about it only from hearsay. These factors, however, are not sufficient to prove an author's hand. His possession of it may have been fortuitous, or he may have come into possession of it and considered publishing it, just as he did another manuscript, which in error he ascribed to Sir Walter Ralegh: the *Cabinet-Council* (1658, while he also was supposedly occupied with *De Doctrina Christiana*).

Introduction

One must also consider the fact that, because of his fame, a large number of works have been erroneously assigned to him, as may be true of *De Doctrina Christiana*. In the article "Attributions" in *A Milton Encyclopedia*, John Shawcross traces over 70 of them (one, for example, is a six-book epic in Latin; another a long tract, *Mans Mortalitie*). Such ascriptions came about "sometimes because of the subject matter, sometimes because of initials attached, sometimes as hoaxes." The manuscript of *De Doctrina Christiana* has a better pedigree than these (though part of the evidence of Milton's authorship of it is his name and initials added to the text only after his death, as will be shown).

The essay that resulted from these early reflections, "The Provenance of the *Christian Doctrine*," I read at the Fourth Milton Symposium, held in Vancouver, British Columbia, in July 1991. Barbara Lewalski and John Shawcross responded with insightful observations and questions. A few months later all three papers appeared in print in *Studies in English Literature*.

The next year, while I was waiting for books to be delivered to my desk in the British Library, it occurred to me to see what I could discover there about Thomas Burgess, Bishop of Winchester, who I vaguely knew had questioned Milton's authoring of the treatise soon after it appeared in 1825. The sole applicable work of Burgess's that the British Library possesses is *Protestant Union*, his edition of Milton's last pamphlet, *Of True Religion*, prefaced by a long argument attacking the ascription of the *Christian*

Doctrine to Milton, in part because its support for manifold heresies would seriously damage his then-great reputation in England. The Bishop chose this pamphlet for reissue because it is one of Milton's strongest anti-Catholic statements, as witness its full title: *Of True Religion, Haeresie, Schism, Toleration, and What Best Means May Be Us'd against the Growth of Popery*. This may be Milton's final, if posthumous, engagement in a public political cause, for in 1826 when Burgess's reprint appeared the major national tension was the issue of enfranchising Roman Catholic citizens.[4] King George IV strongly opposed the move; the Bishop, one of his most fervent supporters, evidently thought that republication of Milton's tract could help this cause.

Its appearance then, of course, had nothing to do with the provenance of the treatise, which purely by chance had been printed in its original Latin text and in an English translation the previous year. Not surprisingly, Burgess employed his long preface to *Of True Religion* to argue against the separate issue of assigning the theological work to Milton. Again by chance, during these years he was president of the Royal Society of Literature, recently founded by and indeed owing its very existence to the support of King George. Because of his position in the Society, Burgess seems to have received full reports of the discovery of the manuscript by Robert Lemon in deposits of what would become the Public Record Office, and of the progress of its editing and translation by Charles Sumner. His position also may have given him prepublication access to the manuscript.

Introduction

Finally, he was one of the best qualified theologians of his day to discuss the Christian heresy of Arianism, which looms so large in the treatise, because he had written a full book on the subject, *Evidence of the Divinity of Christ* (London, 1815) and indeed had founded St. David's College in Wales to counter current Unitarian tendencies there. Besides his preface to Milton's tract, Burgess authored a longer argument, *Milton Contrasted with Milton and with the Scriptures*, which he printed in 1825 for private distribution. What appears to be the sole surviving copy is in the Lampeter Library of St. David's recently reported by James Ogden, along with other books related to Milton from the Bishop's library.[5] Although T.F. Tout, his biographer in the *Dictionary of National Biography*, certainly had access to it (Ogden has privately written me that Tout was a lecturer at St. David's during the 1880s), he shows no interest in its contents beyond its title. Four years later, in 1829, Burgess reprinted *Milton Contrasted with Milton* as the last part of *Milton Not the Author*. The discourses and the reprinted book continued his vigorous attacks against the authenticity of the treatise as Milton's.

And then total silence. Tout concluded that Burgess in these continuing attacks had "exhausted the patience" of the Society, to which the book was addressed by its president. But this is a guess that any reader of the book would recognize at once to be wrong. The Bishop's silence is owing, I think, to the fact that King George himself was publicly identified as a supporter of the authenticity of *De Doctrina*

Christiana. Sumner's work as editor and translator was undertaken at the King's direction; the question of his progress toward publication was even raised in Parliament. Although it is impossible now to document, what happened seems evident: the throne was badly embarrassed by the Bishop's strong arguments against a work it sponsored. The King himself, or one of his advisors, ordered the Bishop to stop, which he did at once. After all, the very existence of the Royal Society of which he was president could have been at risk.

The proof lies in the thoroughness of the censorship visited upon the Bishop. I do not think that a single copy of the 1829 volume survives today in England. At least there is none in the British, Bodleian, or Cambridge Libraries. Nor is there one in the library of the Royal Society, even though the book contains Burgess's presidential reports of the organization for the years 1826, 1827, and 1828. Furthermore, there is no copy of any of Burgess's writings about Milton in the library of Salisbury Cathedral, the Bishop's seat; he evidently deposited these controversial works only in the library of the school he had founded in Wales. I have used a copy that somehow found its way to the public library of Cincinnati, Ohio. Many of the Bishop's ideas appear in the pages that follow, and I have summarized the contents of his Preface and of the book in "The Provenance of the *Christian Doctrine*: Addenda from the Bishop of Salisbury" in *Studies in English Literature* (1993).

The evidence that the Bishop and I have been able to provide to date, however, does not deny with

Introduction

absolute certainty that Milton was the author—nor, on the other hand, has anyone been able to prove that he certainly wrote it. In accepting the work as Milton's, we have merely agreed with unchallenged conclusions drawn a century and a half ago, further discussion then having been cut short by royal censorship. It seems futile to hope that at this late date some decisive primary facts may surface that will finally settle the question. Rather, we must deal with circumstantial evidence, which I shall present. A possible alternative is a linguistic comparison of the Latin of the treatise with the Latin of undoubtedly canonical works. Under such scrutiny would be grammatical, rhetorical, and semantic comparisons. I shall not be concerned with this interesting approach here except for the passage discussing divorce in the treatise.[6] Instead, I shall rely on such circumstantial evidence as can be developed from the manuscript itself and Milton's relationship to it, and as its ideas agree or conflict with those of works that are certainly his. I do not see how one can demonstrate certainty with this method, but it may be persuasive.

When we dismiss the critical accretions to the canon that derive from the treatise, a new understanding of the man and his works emerges. There is certainly less self-contradiction, as Sewell would agree. In this new light Milton stands closer to the great traditions of Christianity, being no longer associated with a merely eccentric fringe. For from the view that accepts *De Doctrina Christiana* as Milton's, his importance to Christian traditions, aside from the current professional analysis of his work, is quite insignificant. I do not know of a single history of Christian dogma that even mentions *De Doctrina Christiana*. We can now read *Paradise Lost* without being lost in combing through endless mazes of theological split hairs, as all western readers could before 1825.

To avoid the necessarily frequent repetition of this title, I have shortened it throughout to its Latin initials, *DDC*. For a similar reason I have abbreviated the titles of three of Milton's tracts published while he supposedly was actively at work on it. *A Treatise of Civil Power in Ecclesiastical Causes* (1659) becomes *Of Civil Power*. *Considerations Touching the Likeliest Means to Remove Hirelings out of the Church* (1659) becomes *Hirelings*, and *Of True Religion, Haeresie, Schism, Toleration*, etc. (1673) becomes *Of True Religion*.

Unless otherwise indicated, all quotations from Milton's prose are from *Complete Prose Works of John Milton* by various editors (New Haven, 1954–1982). Citations are given within parentheses by volume and page, thus (6.666). Every page that follows here testifies to my indebtedness to the English translation of *DDC* by John Carey, to its introductory essays by the late Maurice Kelley, and to his extensive and meticulous notes. All quotations from Milton's poetry are from *The Complete Poetry of John Milton*, ed. John T. Shawcross (New York, 1971). The radical nature of my thesis invites analysis of almost all recent criticism and scholarship which has relied upon *DDC* for its arguments—a very large number. Because it is impossible to consider them all I have

Introduction

briefly taken up only a few representative examples.

My indebtedness is great to those who first gave hearing to my untraditional arguments, which are reproduced here—often in the same words as in the original, though sometimes expanded or rephrased. I especially thank Paul Stanwood, who accepted my first paper on the subject for a panel spot at the Fourth Milton Symposium, held in Vancouver, British Columbia, in July 1991. I am most in debt to Robert Patten, editor of *Studies in English Literature* (*SEL*), who published "The Provenance of the *Christian Doctrine*" with comments by Barbara Lewalski and John Shawcross and my rejoinder in volume 32 (1992), 129–66; "The Provenance of the *Christian Doctrine*: Addenda from the Bishop of Salisbury" in volume 33 (1993), 191–207; and "Animadversions upon the Remonstrants' Defenses against Burgess and Hunter," my response to disagreement with my arguments which the editor had invited from Maurice Kelley and Christopher Hill in volume 34 (1994), 165–203. My thanks are also owing to Professors Kristin McColgan and Charles Durham, who invited me to read "Ramblings in Elucidation of the Authorship of the *Christian Doctrine*" at the Second Southeastern Milton Conference held in Murfreesboro, Tennessee, in October 1993 and who since have published it in their collection of papers from that conference, *Arenas of Conflict*, 41–50. They also gave me a place on the program for the third such conference in 1995 to read a paper analyzing the discussion of divorce in *DDC*. It has not been printed until now.

Last, but by no means least, I am indebted more

Introduction

than I can say to several leading Miltonists whose comments have forced me to clarify my own thinking and to ground my arguments more firmly. This is not to say that they agree with my conclusions, only that they have responded thoughtfully and constructively to my arguments. They are John Shawcross, emeritus of the University of Kentucky; Paul Sellin, emeritus of the University of California in Los Angeles; Robert T. Fallon, emeritus of La Salle University; Anthony Low of New York University; and Gordon Campbell of the University of Leicester, England. Without their help I could not have proceeded. For advice about problems of Renaissance Latin, I am indebted to David Wharton of the Classics Department of the University of North Carolina in Greensboro. Finally, the keen editorial eye of my friend and former student, James O. Allsup, has been invaluable in exorcising the demons that plague one's clarity and style.

Chapter One

Milton's Funeral and the Disposition of His Manuscripts

John Milton was buried in St. Giles Church, near London's Cripplegate, on 12 November 1674. It is located in the cultural center known today as the Barbican. During intermissions theatre and concert goers there can face across a moat this ancient edifice, an anomaly amidst the modern buildings that surround and dwarf it. John Aubrey, who collected contemporary information for a biography of Milton, guessed that the English cartographer and antiquary John Speed and he "lie together" at the upper end of the chancel,[1] although by Aubrey's time in the early 1680s the commemorative stone had been removed because of remodeling. Visitors from across the moat, however, can easily locate its placement today near the lectern on the left side.[2] But Milton would not be permitted to lie quietly. In 1790 some ghoulish pranksters broke into the grave and put the skeleton on view for a couple of days before it was reinterred (less, it seems, some bones, teeth, and locks of hair).³ Then in our own century German bombs destroyed the entire area in 1940, leaving only the nave and spire of the church. Everything now, however, has been put again to rights; its quiet stance across the moat invites a visit.

Because Artillery Walk, the location of Milton's last residence in London, was in the St. Giles parish, burial in its chancel seems natural until one reflects that its services were certainly Anglican. The officiating priest could not have conducted them if Milton had made himself known in the neighborhood as a self-declared heretic.⁴ Had he dictated *DDC*, whose author declared—with God as his witness—that he planned to make public this, his "dearest and best possession" (6.121), he must have been unaccountably silent with his neighbors about its contents—at a time when Christopher Hill thinks he was a regular denizen of the social meetings then equivalent to those of a local pub today.⁵

Furthermore, burial in St. Giles must have been in accord with Milton's own desires expressed to his family,⁶ for dissenting Puritans were ordinarily interred then in Bunhill Fields, closer and, in fact, immediately adjacent to his home on Artillery Walk. It is not enough to conclude that Milton desired burial in St. Giles only because his father had been buried there in 1647. He has been so thoroughly characterized as a Puritan that one tends to forget that his polemics were hurled against the government—the polity—of the Church, not against its theological dogmas. His allusion to its mortuary observations in

Hirelings (7.298-99) inveighs against priests who accept payment for such services, not against the form of the service itself.

More important, several of his later writings reveal forthright agreement with certain Anglican practices. In *Paradise Lost* Adam and Eve's morning prayer (5.153-208), though supposedly "unmeditated" (5.149; *DDC* concludes that "the church has no need of a liturgy" 6.670), is in fact a paraphrase of part of the morning service in the Book of Common Prayer, "O all ye works of the Lord, bless ye the Lord," even including a modification of the Prayerbook's liturgical refrain, "Praise him, and magnify him forever," in its varying repetitions of "praise" in lines 172-204.[7]

Again, in *Paradise Regained* at the baptism of Jesus God announces from heaven that his Son's "weakness shall o'recome Satanic strength/And all the world and mass of sinful flesh" (1.161-62), exactly as a person baptised according to the Book of Common Prayer, or his representative, promises to "renounce the devil and all his works, the vain pomp and glory of the world, with all covetous desires of the same, and the sinful desires of the flesh." The tripartite directive is identical in the service and in these lines of the poem that derive from it; neither originates from the baptismal accounts in the gospels. The poem that follows shows Jesus obeying these three renunciations in the temptations in the wilderness.[8] Again, Milton's last public pamphlet, *Of True Religion* (1673), is addressed to an Anglican, not Puritan, audience. As Daniel Doerksen has recently observed, Milton in this tract identified with the

Anglican communion as "Our church" (8.434)[9] and refers approvingly to several of its Thirty-nine Articles (8.419–20). Although I do not know of any study that closely analyzes how many of the Articles Milton's works are concerned with, it seems that (unless he authored *DDC*) he could accept all of them except the few concerned with church polity, specifically No. 23 (Of Ministering in the Congregation), No. 26 (Of the Consecration of Bishops and Ministers), and No. 37 (Of the Power of the Civil Magistrate). Problematic of his acceptance are No. 20 (Of the Authority of the Church) and No. 34 (Of the Traditions of the Church). One must conclude that he was buried an Anglican communicant, the service being the "Order for the Dead" of the Book of Common Prayer. His "puritanism" extended only to church governance, not doctrine.

He did not leave a written will. Court records show that he told his brother, Christopher, and a servant, Elizabeth Fisher, how he wanted his estate to be distributed. There are no directions for the disposition of his books, manuscripts or other literary remains.[10] The early biographer Aubrey reported that his young widow gave such property to one of his nephews, Edward Phillips, whom he had tutored years before.[11]

Somehow two major manuscripts found another disposition, turning up in the possession of a new Cambridge graduate, Daniel Skinner.[12] (He may have gotten hold of some others as well, which would later surface in different hands—the *Commonplace Book* now in the British Library and the notebook now in the library of Trinity College, Cambridge; but they do not concern us here.) I shall detail later the circumstances so far as they can be recovered that led to Skinner's procurement of them. One manuscript was his transcription of many (but not all) of the State Papers originating with Milton's work for the Commonwealth and the Protectorate; the other is the copy of *DDC*, the first 196 pages of which he also transcribed. His purpose was evidently to publish both in England, but if so he was not successful—in the case of the State Papers because no Restoration licensing authority would sanction such Interregnum documents and possibly in the case of *DDC* because of its heretical contents.

Skinner then explored publication abroad, sending both manuscripts to Daniel Elzevir in Amsterdam, who at first viewed them favorably. But Sir Joseph Williamson, Secretary of State, intervened to block the publication of the State Papers, seemingly having heard of Skinner's goals from the naive Skinner himself. Elzevir may also have stopped because of a competitive publication of them as *Literae Pseudo-Senatûs* in 1676 by the publisher Blaeu, also located in Amsterdam. As for his printing *DDC*, he seems to have consulted Philip van Limborch, a noted Dutch theologian, who advised against it on the basis of its manifest heresy of Arianism.[13]

Although Skinner promised to return the manuscript of the politically suspect State Papers, his father, Daniel, Sr., intervened in the winter of 1676–77 to demand that Elzevir return everything to him. This the publisher did as soon as spring weather permitted. When the elder Skinner received them,

Visitation Unimplor'd

he sent both to Sir Joseph, who in turn stored them among state records which in time would become part of today's Public Record Office. There they remained until Robert Lemon, Deputy Keeper, came across them as he was cataloguing its documents in 1823. Recognizing the importance of *DDC* to a public that esteemed Milton as its greatest poet, he identified it as Milton's by its association with his State Papers and because of the record of the existence of such a treatise by the early biographers. At first he erroneously assumed that the Skinner who had last possessed the manuscripts was Milton's student and friend, the well-known Cyriack, rather than Daniel. The news of the discovery was hailed as of such great national importance that King George himself directed that it be edited and published as soon as possible; two volumes, one of text, the other of translation, accordingly appeared in 1825, the work of Charles Sumner.

Chapter Two

The Evidence of the Early Biographers

Major support to prove that Milton wrote *DDC* comes from the early biographers. All six of them—Aubrey's "Minutes" (1681), the Anonymous Life (early 1680s?, generally assumed to have been written by Milton's pupil and friend Cyriack Skinner), and the lives by Anthony à Wood (1691), Edward Phillips (1694), John Toland (1698) and Jonathan Richardson (1734)—state in almost complete conformity with one another (except Phillips, who will be treated separately) that Milton was occupied at one time or another with such a work.[1] Those by Wood, Toland, and Richardson, however, can be ignored here because on the subject of the treatise the latter two merely repeat Wood's information which, in turn, derives directly and solely from Aubrey and the Anonymous Life. These two alone accordingly demand attention.

Aubrey provides minimal but important and authentic information about the existence of the manuscript of *DDC*: he had learned of an "Idea Theologiae in MS in the hands of Mr. Skinner, a merchant's sonne, in Marke Lane" (9–10). Although factually true a few years earlier, as we have seen, the manuscript by Aubrey's day had actually been removed from Daniel's possession for deposit among the public records. Aubrey's information, that is, was accurate but dated. Furthermore, he did not know either the correct title of the work or Daniel's first name. Thus when Wood came to use this information (furnished by Aubrey) he assumed in error that the "Skinner" who had possessed the manuscript was the better-known Cyriack. One may conclude that Aubrey had not seen the manuscript, knew no details of its contents, and learned about its existence only at a somewhat distant second hand that originated from the Daniel Skinner family.

The Anonymous Biographer, the other primary source, also possessed important information: after Milton's blindness had relieved him from most of his public duties for the Commonwealth (that is, sometime after early 1652)

> hee began ... a *Latin Thesaurus* ...; Also the composing *Paradise Lost*. And the framing a *Body of Divinity* out of the Bible: All which, notwithstanding the several Calamities befalling him in his fortunes, hee finish'd after the Restoration.

He goes on to list as also completed then the *History of Britain, Paradise Regained, Samson Agonistes*, the *Logic*, and the *Grammar*. Finally, he knew that Milton had begun a Greek thesaurus (29).

If, as seems probable from the handwriting, the Anonymous Biographer was Milton's friend and former student Cyriack Skinner,[2] he had the opportunity to know at first hand details of Milton's life that he chronicled in this biography, though the degree of their intimacy seems to have varied considerably over the years. After Milton returned from Italy he established in his home a private school in which Cyriack was enrolled. Born in 1627, the young man was aged 15 to 20 between 1642 and 1647 while he was one of Milton's pupils, just the period during which, as Parker has pointed out, the anonymous biography is especially complete.[3] It is wrong about some details relating to the tracts that Milton published during these years, but these are minor errors easily explained by tricks of memory following the passage of well over 30 years when Skinner set them down and by the fact that no one had yet compiled a formal list of Milton's publications. The years from 1647 to 1654 are likewise well covered, if perhaps not in so great detail. Milton's attacks on the King, his *Defenses* of the Commonwealth and of himself, and his blindness with increasing dependence upon amanuenses chronicled here all seem to derive from personal observations made during this period.

Following 1654, however, the biography is far less intimate, scarcely unexpected as Skinner was establishing his own household. Now he reports in the very general terms already quoted Milton's activities, literary and otherwise, with some large gaps. The years 1658–1660, when the evidence of his "amenuensis" Jeremie Picard reveals his special concern for

DDC, are almost completely omitted. The biography does not mention the two tracts of 1659 (*Of True Religion* and *Hirelings*) and the two editions of *Readie and Easie Way* the next spring. Indeed, the narrative is bare until the Restoration at the end of May that year, when its author reports that Milton lost £2000 at the failure of the Excise Bank (32). Shortly before, on 5 May, the record survives that Milton transferred a bond for £400 to Cyriack, though the biography does not mention this fact. The amanuensis Picard was a witness to this transaction and thus Cyriack must have met him.[4] Although Edward Phillips, the nephew, included Cyriack among a group of Milton's friends (74), he names him especially in connection with the two sonnets to Cyriack which date most probably in 1655. The lack of evidence points to a gap in the close association between Milton and his pupil-friend from about 1656 to May 1660, key dates for work on the treatise. Then the approaching Restoration of the monarchy placed Milton in potential peril and friends like Cyriack rallied to his assistance.

Furthermore, except on a single point, the anonymous biography showed no specific knowledge of the contents of *DDC*. Its author had, however, heard vaguely that it supported heretical doctrines, a rumor that he questioned. Arguing from "so Christian a Life, so great Learning, and so unbyass'd a search after Truth" as Milton's had been, he thought it improbable that "any errors in Doctrine should spring." But, having learned something of its heretical contents, he concludes, therefore his Judgment in his Body of Divinity concerning some speculative points, differing perhaps from that commonly receiv'd, (and which is thought to bee the reason that [it] never was printed) neither ought rashly to bee condemnd, and however himselfe not to bee uncharitably censur'd (31).

Because, as has been seen, only Daniel Skinner had tried to publish the work in Holland and perhaps failed because of its eccentric contents, the most likely source of the rumor that Cyriack picked up was that of the earlier possessor of the manuscript, Daniel. But these sentences from the anonymous biography reveal no direct knowledge of any details of the work that its author heard from either the *DDC*'s author or its copyist, Picard.

For one specific detail, however, the biographer surprisingly does have first-hand and convincing evidence of familiarity. In his summary of Milton's divorce tracts of the earlier 1640s, and quite separate from his report about a "Body of Divinity," he wrote that Milton interpreted the apparent denial of divorce by the New Testament evangelists as "rectifying the abuses of it; rendring to that purpose another Sense of the word Fornication (and wch is also the Opinion amongst others of Mr. Selden in his *Uxor Hebraea*) then what is commonly receivd" (23). But this could not have been Cyriack's memory from his school days; Selden's book would not be printed until two years after Milton's. Rather, the anonymous biography seems in this single instance almost to be quoting directly from the passage supporting divorce in book 1, chapter 10 of *DDC*: "as Selden demonstrated particularly well in his *Uxor Hebraea*..., the word *fornication*... does not mean only *adultery*. It can also mean either what is called *some shameful thing*... or it can signify" anything at variance with marital happiness as "I have proved... elsewhere... and Selden has demonstrated the same thing" (6.378). The passage from the biography so accurately echoes the one from the treatise that it seems clear its author picked it up directly from *DDC*'s author—or, at least, the author of that part of its chapter 10—or from Milton's amanuensis in the passage, Picard, who witnessed the business transaction with Cyriack early in May 1660.

Thus Cyriack could truthfully assert that Milton was the author of at least this part of chapter 10 of the "Body of Divinity." Yet it is surprising that this is the sole specific detail in the entire work that he knew of. His statement that Milton framed it "out of the Bible" is not accurate (it was framed out of Wolleb's *Compendium* with supporting biblical quotations, as will appear later in this chapter); one may question whether Milton indeed finished it "after the Restoration"; and his knowledge of its supposed heresies is quite fuzzy. All that is probable—and this seems assured—is that his evidence shows Milton to have been directly associated with the passage on divorce, a subject to which I shall return in chapter 9. I conclude that Cyriack's knowledge otherwise of Milton's activities from 1656 to May 1660 is tenuous at best. Except for the single specific detail in the section on divorce, his information came from rumors seeming to have originated from Daniel's abortive attempts to publication.

I conclude, then, that (except for Edward Phillips and for the Anonymous Biographer's specific but limited knowledge of the passage on divorce in chapter 10) all the early biographers owe their information about the existence of an "Idea Theologiae" or a "Body of Divinity" to rumors, specifically to Daniel Skinner's publicizing the existence and something of the contents of the manuscript, which he had recently tried to publish. The authenticity of his information will become an issue when we turn to his role as its possessor and copyist. There remains to be considered the important and first-hand testimony of Edward Phillips.

In his "Life," prefixed to his translation of many of the State Papers and several sonnets, Phillips describes in some detail the private school where he had been "wholly committed to [Milton's] Charge and Care" (60), the same routine that Cyriack Skinner, three years his senior, had followed. Having outlined its rigorous classical and linguistic regime, he reports that each *Sunday's* work was for the most part the Reading each day a Chapter of the *Greek* Testament, and hearing his Learned Exposition upon the same." This was followed by "the writing from his own dictation, some part, from time to time, of a Tractate which he thought fit to collect from the ablest of Divines, who had written on the subject; *Amesius, Wollebius,* &c. *viz.* A perfect System of Divinity, of which more hereafter" (61).[5] Unhappily, Phillips never returned to carry out the promise of his last sentence, nor does he mention the subject in the detailed paragraph concerned with the important years 1658–1660, though he refers accurately in it to *Of Civil Power, Hirelings* and *Readie and Easie Way* as well as personal details like two changes of his residence. These are the specific observations of a close acquaintance that are quite different from the generalized reports of these years by the Anonymous Biographer. Another proof of his intimacy can be found in the entry in his own handwriting in Aubrey's "Minutes": "*Edw. Philips his chief Amanuensis*" for dictating *Paradise Lost* (7), which included these years. He knew about Milton's long-continued work on an unpublished Latin thesaurus, dated by the Anonymous Biographer as coinciding with work on the "Body of Divinity." Had Milton been working then on *DDC*, it would have ranked (as it does) as his most ambitious current project and so, one would think, must have come to Phillips's attention. But he makes no suggestion of a return to such a treatise as Milton had had his students write in the 1640s. Such lack of allusion, of course, does not constitute proof that Milton was not so employed, though it surely is strongly suggestive.

If we accept for the moment Phillips's report of the students' occupation on Sundays in creating "a Tractate which he thought fit to collect from the ablest of Divines, who had written on the subject; *Amesius, Wollebius,* &c." it is not "out of the Bible" as the Anonymous Biographer had been led to believe but out of the doctrinal summaries of these two authors. The thousands of proof texts were added to prove the truth of passages derived from them. The manuscript that we now have requires one moderate change of emphasis: Ames does not share equally with Wolleb as its formative source, although his *Medulla* certainly ranks very high among books cited.[6] The major model for the work that we now have is Wolleb's *Compendium*.[7] Kelley has argued for Ames as formative in that "Milton [i.e., the author of *DDC*], like Ames, divides his work into two books" (6.18). So too does Wolleb, whose work, like *DDC*, has 50 chapters all told (but divided 36 + 14 versus *DDC*'s 33 + 17). Ames has 63 (divided 41 + 22). Although details in them vary considerably, book 1, chapter 3 in both *DDC* and Wolleb concern Divine Decrees (chapter 7 in Ames). Chapter 4 in both is on Predestination (chapter 25 in Ames). Chapters 9 and 10 of *DDC* match 7 and 8 of Wolleb on the government of angels and man, and so on. That is, Ames's overall organization is not nearly so close to that of *DDC* as is Wolleb's. Furthermore, from early on the author of *DDC* quotes directly and frequently from the *Compendium*; examples begin with Kelley's second note in chapter 1 (6.128) and continue to appear frequently to the end of the work.

I conclude that *DDC* as we now have it originates primarily from Wolleb's book, though this is not at all to argue that Ames's was not within its author's view too. Kelley demonstrates verbal parallels between the *Medulla* and *DDC*, book 1, chapter 2 (6.129, notes 10 and 11) and frequently thereafter. But book 2 of *DDC* quotes Ames's work only once (6.706) with possibly a few other allusions there (see Kelley's notes to 6.707, 712, and 713), whereas this later part of the treatise teems with direct quotations from the *Compendium*.[8] The slight change of emphasis in Phillips's narration I have suggested here in no way casts any doubt on the general validity of his report about the Sunday activities in Milton's school.

If we recognize the primary influence throughout *DDC* of the *Compendium*, we seem to have in the generally overlooked book 2 of the treatise passages that survive essentially unchanged from the earlier form of the work in the 1640s: statements directly quoted or very closely paraphrased from Wolleb's book, followed by supporting biblical proof texts but with little or no authorial comment. Chapter 2 consists only of such material, emended by a couple of sentences of additional interpretation (6.651); chapter 3 is made up only of Wolleb's statement and supportive proof texts, as is chapter 8. Similar textual compilations constitute chapters 9, 10, 11, 12, 15 and 16. Having perceived this original basic construction, one can glance through the other chapters of book 2 to recognize an underlying Wolleb/proof text foundation that has been overlaid with authorial additions more or less extensive depending upon interest in the topic. In chapter 1, for example, the subject of good works and individual merit raised by Wolleb receives a long expansion that analyzes the Roman Catholic dogma of the Church's Treasury of good works and of the worth of one's merits (6.643–45). Because of this recognizable overlaying, it is possible to distinguish an earlier stratum whose creation Phillips reported and that became the basis for the construction of all of book 2 as we have it. By extension, though much of the underlying fabric is now hidden, the same is probably true of book 1 as a kind of palimpsest. Its chapters 15, 18, 19 and 32 evidence a similar origin in Wolleb. Indeed, Kelley has argued for just such an early (but orthodox) stage of composition followed by a second (but heterodox) work overlaying the first (6.19–22). Such a history of the development of the manuscript in Milton's hands also seems to be entirely convincing and buttressed by Phillips's memories—except that I find it impossible to imagine Milton, a Cambridge graduate embroiled in national arguments over church polity and divorce, occupied with so rudimentary a project as fitting proof texts to sentences quoted or paraphrased from Wolleb's elementary compendium. I also question whether Milton would remember the activities of his late thirties as the author of the "Epistle" prefacing the treatise does his:

> I began by devoting myself when I was a boy [adolescens] to an earnest study of the Old and New Testaments in their original languages, and then proceeded to go carefully through some of the shorter systems of theologians (6.119),

like Ames and Wolleb. But as "adolescens" Milton could not have procured a copy of the *Medulla* until 1623 and of the *Compendium* until 1626. Both were printed on the Continent. Editions of the former in 1627 and 1629 showed its growth in popularity late in the decade. Wolleb's book, the more important one, was not reprinted until 1634, 1638, and 1642—well after Milton had received both degrees. The statement quoted here from the treatise, on the other hand, would perfectly match the memory of a student in Milton's little academe when both books were already well established for student use.

Let us again consider Phillips's words: on Sundays Milton's pupils wrote "from his own dictation . . . a treatise." From this sentence it has been generally assumed that he was using them to create his own treatise, presumably this early form of *DDC*. Phillips's meaning, however, may be quite different. He had already observed that Milton might better have preserved his eyesight "had he not . . . been perpetually busied in his own Laborious Undertakings of the Book or Pen" (60). He did his own work at this period, that is, and did not rely upon his students as amanuenses. Furthermore, the sentence about their "writing from his own dictation . . . a Tractate" is in the context of their continuing education on Sundays, not that of his own projects, which Phillips later treats separately. I suggest that their individual Sunday assignments were for each to create his own "Tractate" at Milton's "dictation"—that is, at his "authoritative direction," a meaning well established in Phillips's time. Or in a literal reading, as Paul Sellin has suggested to me, he is giving them practice in writing the Latin that he reads aloud from Wolleb as the basic outline for a religious tractate that each is to expand and annotate for himself. One can still admire such an educational program—a fine propaedeutic for his students, but one that only a "pupil-teacher" whom he scorned (2.608) would undertake for himself. In *Doctrine and Discipline*, which dates from these years of his private school, he indeed has left from his classroom his own evaluation of the elementary nature of Ames's *Medulla*: Milton judges that his achievements will not be recognized by his prejudiced opponents, "whose capacity since their youth run ahead into the easie creek of a system or a Medulla," and so who display their "unlabour'd rudiments" in refusing him recognition (2.232–33).[9] So I conclude that the treatise we have began in the assignment for each student to make such a compilation, and to develop his own religious digest from Wolleb with frequent reference to Ames and others ("&c."), buttressed with his collection of biblical proof texts.

But the work as we now know it, especially book 1, goes far beyond the presumably safe orthodoxy of Milton's classes to the heterodoxy that overlays much of it. This derives, as I shall later show, solely from continental, not English sources. If the copy of *DDC* that we have did indeed originate in this way as an assignment in Milton's school, its author, whoever he was, must have gone abroad to continue his education, where he came under the influence of continental authorities of decidedly radical dogmatic doctrines. The work does not have the slightest suggestion of an association with either of the English universities. As will become clear, his most probable locations were in the Low Countries and in Saumur, France. Across the Channel he would meet followers of free-thinking religious leaders like Socinus and Arminius, who became much more significant to the young man than the conservative Reformed divines like Ames and Wolleb upon whose thought he had based his earlier florilegium under Milton's direction. Not surprisingly, many of his additions to this early text disagree with their statements, which he now takes as points of departure. But because a copy of his manuscript, made as we shall see by Jeremie Picard, later appeared in Milton's possession, it somehow found its way back, most probably by its author's return to England and his old teacher in the 1650s, bringing with him his now much-elaborated schoolboy exercise. Its elementary origins still show through quite clearly, especially in book 2. If this projection is correct, one can assume Milton's continuing interest in his former pupil and his new views. Such a double residence by the author of *DDC*, in England with Milton and then on the Continent, can account for the two distinct forms in which the treatise has come down to us: a simplistic and elementary collection of quotations from Wolleb supplemented by Ames and filled out by proof texts; and a complex, much longer response to such earlier naiveté which has been written over many chapters of that original. But who he was I see no means of discovering. The copyist Picard? The otherwise unidentified former student, Mr. Packer, whom Aubrey knew (9)? We can conclude that something happened to him: he died or left England, perhaps as a *persona non grata* after the Restoration in late May 1660, for there is no evidence of any association of Picard, who originally copied the entire work, with Milton thereafter.

The Early Biographers

In any case, with Charles's return, the blind polemecist's life for months became chaotic. Daniel Skinner's recopying of the first 196 pages as we shall see has obliterated changes that anyone may have made on Picard's copy, but the rest, by Picard, does have a great many emendations by a variety of hands—variety that suggests the dictation of a blind man. But despite their number the alterations are all of a minor nature—improvements, not major revisions such as an original author would make. If Milton indeed dictated most or all of them, he made no effort to emend its dogmas with which he disagreed, like predestination or the continuing authority of Old Testament moral laws. The copy remained in Milton's possession until his death. The simplest explanation of all these facts is that the unknown author had been an esteemed friend of Milton (possibly a former student) who for some reason (death may be the most likely) could no longer work on his great projected religious treatise. In his memory, Milton carefully preserved his manuscript and dictated over the years a considerable number of what he regarded as minor improvements and with at least one major addition as will appear later, a more extensive addition to book 1, chapter 10. There may be others. He also may have had publication in mind and, in the absence of its author, assumed full responsibility for the work.

Chapter Three

The Two Scribes

The manuscript of *DDC*, now in the Public Record Office in London, survives in two clearly distinguishable hands. One copied pages 1–196 (which end with the close of book 1, chapter 14), 308, and 571–74. The second is reponsible for all the rest. There are corrections and interlineations by Hand One throughout the work of Hand Two, but none of Hand Two in that of Hand One. Thus it is a safe assumption that Hand Two originally wrote out the entire work and that Hand One copied from it the pages listed here, discarding all the originals by Hand Two except page 308, which survives in duplicate. Hand One probably did this work to prepare a cleaner copy, perhaps for a printer; for the surviving pages by Hand Two have numerous changes, some made by Hand One but others by half-a-dozen or more yet unidentified scribes. There are some alterations in the pages owing to Hand One, but they have all been recognized as having been made after the discovery of the manuscript in 1823. Hand One is not only later; it postdates completion of the entire work in the form that has come down to us.[1]

The original work of Hand Two, however, was itself copied from an antecedent manuscript, for its relatively final accuracy at times reveals anticipation that would be made only by someone copying material from an earlier draft.[2] The original discoverer of the manuscript, Robert Lemon, and its editor and translator, Charles Sumner, thought at first that Hand Two was that of Milton's nephew, also author of one of the early biographies mentioned, Edward Phillips. This identification they deduced from his statement in Aubrey's "Minutes" (cited above) that he himself was the main amanuensis for Milton's dictation of *Paradise Lost* which, they believed, proceeded contemporaneously with the transcription of *DDC* (and Milton's supposed dictation of it), dated, as will appear, around 1658 to 1660. But it is now certain that Phillips's handwriting was not that of Hand Two nor was he even one of the amanuenses who helped emend the pages that Hand Two had copied. Indeed, Phillips seems not to have worked at all on the treatise—another piece of evidence to distance Milton from it—since at just that time he was dictating the poem to his nephew.

Not until the 1920s did James Holly Hanford prove on the basis of handwriting that an otherwise unknown Jeremie Picard was responsible for the pages set down by Hand Two.[3] He identified it from signatures on documents associated with Milton between

January 1658 and May 1660 (the last is the conveyance of the bond to Cyriack Skinner mentioned earlier). Picard also made a few late entries in the Commonplace Book and transcribed Sonnet 23 to a page added to Milton's notebook, now located in the Library of Trinity College, Cambridge. (He wrote the heading too for these additions.) Sotheby identified the notebook's paper as deriving from the same stock as that used for some of the pages of *DDC* that Picard transcribed.[4] If the sonnet, "Me thought I saw my late espoused saint," refers to Katherine Woodcock, Milton's second wife (I think it does), she died on 3 February 1658, providing an occasion for the poem that accords very well with the dates of the association between Picard and Milton that Hanford discovered. Finally, John Shawcross may have found Picard at work earlier, in May 1655, for Cromwell's envoy, Samuel Morland.[5]

Yet Picard remains a shadowy figure, possibly to be identified as the otherwise unknown "Mr. Packer" already mentioned, whom Aubrey named as one of Milton's private students in the 1640s. William Elton also located a Jeremiah Pickard or Piskard who entered Bethlehem Hospital in London (for the insane) in 1700. He may be the same as the unnamed "secretary of the well-known Milton" whom a German traveler, Adam Ebert, reported seeing there as a patient in 1678.[6] It is difficult today to evaluate adequately this fragmentary evidence. The one certainty is that there is no record of any association between Milton and Picard after the Restoration of the monarchy at the end of May 1660. In the ensuing chaos of Milton's household this may not be surprising.

I think that search for his identity should also be made on the Continent; for, as will appear in the next chapter, many of the authorities cited in *DDC* were located there. In the Netherlands I have indeed located a Jeronimus Pickaert, who was a minor landscape painter. He was born in Rotterdam in 1628, was in Middelburg in 1649, in Leiden in 1655, again in Rotterdam in 1659, and in Amsterdam in 1674.[7] Despite tensions between England and Holland during these years, there was some travel between the two countries. Milton was involved in political negotiations between them from 1651 to 1654,[8] and his American friend Roger Williams may have been teaching him Dutch at this time.[9] Except for possession of the right name, however, this Dutch Pickaert remains a vague and unhelpful figure who must be ignored, unless some more persuasive evidence should surface.

In the many pages of the surviving manuscript for which Picard was responsible there are additions, redactions, and corrections that run into the hundreds. Maurice Kelley has minutely examined and classified them.[10] They tend to be short and, as noted above, never involve fundamental revisions of doctrine. From their characteristic writing patterns, Kelley has identified seven different hands and thinks that there may be more.[11] An obvious implication is that a blind or otherwise handicapped person would have to rely on a number of assistants for work on his text. Milton, of course, was blind—important evidence for his authorial responsibility. But let us examine this evidence in detail.

Whenever the order of entry of an emendation can be determined, it seems clear that Picard himself made all the earliest changes and was then followed by the various anonymous hands. I conclude from Kelley's enumeration[12] that about 560 are owing to Picard. In particular, he amplified dogma 42 times and rewrote 5 pages (300–04). None of the anonymous amanuenses approach such numbers or such significance for their contents, evidence that he may have been the original author. The preponderance of examples of Picard's activity indicates that Milton (if he did dictate some changes) was most involved with the manuscript only between 1658 and 1660, the limited period of their association. One must also remember that Picard had copied the entire manuscript—no small chore—even before he entered any of Milton's emendations or corrections. After 1660 Milton would have had to rely on others to enter the emendations which are made less frequently.

I think it unlikely, but possible, that Picard would have recopied a complete manuscript Milton had made in his youth ("adolescens") or as a teacher in his late thirties. But it is impossible that anyone could dictate in the late 1650s a work of the size and complexity of *DDC*, have someone copy the entire corpus with its mixture of conservative and radical doctrines, and then dictate additional emendations before that amanuensis left him in 1660. Far more likely is that Picard (or "Packer"?) copied his own work begun under Milton's tutelage and amplified abroad under religiously eccentric authorities, or that he copied the work of someone now unknown to us, producing a manuscript that the blind man felt obliged to improve modestly, because its author no longer could do so.

We know a great deal more about the later copyist, Daniel Skinner of Hand One. He certainly possessed the manuscript of *DDC* after Milton's death; he transcribed a good many of its pages and tried to publish it in Holland, and he was the main source of information about it for all of the early biographers except Edward Phillips. Phillips's report concerning any religious treatise dates, as we have seen, only from his early life as one of Milton's pupils, despite the fact that he had ample opportunity to witness dictation of such a treatise if it happened in the later 1650s.[13] Daniel Skinner's testimony, transmitted at second hand to the biographers, has been unquestioningly accepted as authentic and as the major evidence that the work was Milton's. This assumes that he was one of the later amanuenses, working under Milton's direction for an extended time in copying out for publication the text of the State Papers that, along with *DDC*, he also certainly possessed and that is entirely in his hand.

Skinner was born about 1651 into the family of a well-to-do London merchant and entered Trinity College, Cambridge, on 1 July 1670, from which he graduated in 1674.[14] There is no record of any association with Milton until two years after the poet's death (November 1674) when Skinner himself claimed, in a letter to his friend Samuel Pepys, that he had "happen'd to be acquainted with Milton in his lifetime, (which out of mere love to learning I procur'd, and noe other concern ever pass'd betwixt us but a great desire and ambition for some of his learning)."[15] There is certainly no sense of intimacy here nor any suggestion that Skinner had served as Milton's amanuensis, as has been assumed from his postmortem possession of the State Papers and *DDC* manuscripts. He goes on to claim that he has "the works of Milton which he left behind him to me," a statement that both Masson and Parker took to imply that Milton made this recent graduate his literary executor (though Parker adds that "there were a number of Milton's friends and acquaintances who were obviously more competent to arrange for publication abroad").[16]

But, sadly, Skinner is not a reliable witness when testifying on his own behalf—as he does here to explain his possession of what he accurately judged to be valuable manuscripts even though, by the date of his writing to Pepys, he had been unable to find a publisher for either.[17] French has discovered an unsigned letter by a knowledgeable contemporary who wrote: "I am informed that since the death of Mr. Milton his Books have byn lookt over by one Mr. Skinner a scholar and a bold young man who has cull'd out what he thought fitt, amongst the rest he has taken a manuscript of Mr. Milton's written on the Civil Ecclesiastical Government of the Kingdom which he is resolved to print."[18] Although he appears to have confused the subjects of the two manuscripts, it seems probable that this correspondent's information is otherwise reliable.

I am concerned to distance Skinner from Milton because, as I have shown in my discussion of the early biographers, his testimony is a major source in identifying Milton as the author of *DDC*. I am not questioning that he honestly believed the work Milton's, but I question whether he was close enough to the subject to know the truth about it. It was, of course, in his interest to believe that Milton was the author, but as he wrote Pepys, "no other concern ever pass'd between us." Before Milton's death he seems to have had only a Cambridge undergraduate's interest in knowing one of its famous graduates.

His transcription of the State Papers has led to the widespread assumption that he made it at Milton's direction in preparation for publication of them, which was projected to accompany the *Epistolarum Familiarium*, the latter of which actually appeared in print in May 1674. If he indeed made this copy, Skinner must have known him for many months before his death the following November and so presumably would have been able to speak with authority on the authorship of *DDC*. But censorship barred inclusion of the State Papers in the book; Milton replaced them with his early college exercises, the *Prolusions*, which filled out the volume. Everyone has naturally believed that Skinner "retained the [rejected] manuscript that he had made"[19] to accompany *Epistolarum Familiarium* and that he then tried to publish through Daniel Elzevir in Holland, along with *DDC*.

Such a projected lengthy association between Skinner and Milton based on this history of the State

Papers is, however, tenuous at best. Someone else—a name now totally lost to history—had copied them too, because a collection of the Papers made independently of Skinner's was published twice on the Continent in 1676 as *Literae Pseudo-Senatûs Anglicani Cromwellii* (to Skinner's intense dissatisfaction). Its compiler has never been identified, and it has been assumed that he made his transcriptions from Milton's originals after Milton's death with the goal of the successful publication in 1676. Robert Fallon, the major authority on the subject, writes: "most scholars agree that [Skinner's manuscript] is the original one prepared for the volume *Epistolarum*."[20] But that Skinner's manuscript was not the one prepared under Milton's direction for that publication seems clear from one important fact: Skinner could not date several letters (nos. 112–22) that the transcription of *Literae* places in nearly correct order.[21] Another amanuensis who did get the approximate dates directly from Milton must have been responsible for the collection, which was prepared under its author's direction for the *Epistolarum* volume of 1674. I think that, after censorship forbade its inclusion, this unknown amanuensis managed to place it abroad two years later as *Literae*. According to Skinner's own testimony the agent for this transaction was Moses Pitt (or Pitts).[22] Although understandably irritated by this successful publication of the competing text of the State Papers, Skinner admitted that its transcriber had his material directly from Milton, if "surreptitiously."[23]

Skinner, we must conclude, managed somehow to

copy on his own after their author's death those letters which now constitute his manuscript in the Public Record Office—copies which John Shawcross also tentatively dates as having been made in 1675.[24] In conclusion, Skinner's assumed lengthy intimacy with Milton—by which he would certainly have known him to be the author of *DDC*—cannot be proved from his transcriptions of the State Papers. There is no other evidence. He would seem to have named Milton as the author of the treatise only because he had procured the manuscript from among his possessions after his death, perhaps as a purchase from Phillips, to whom, according to Aubrey his widow "gave all his papers." Daniel's father was a successful merchant who seems to have been eager to help his son, just graduated from the university, get a good position. Publication of it and of the State Papers he may have judged supportive, though ironically Daniel could place neither and, indeed, his very possession of the State Papers at this time proved to be a handicap.

Although the date is uncertain when Skinner worked on his partial transcription of *DDC*, probably to clean up the text for publication,[25] it would have been after Milton's death, as Kelley thinks (6.38). He was simultaneously transcribing the State Papers with the same goal in mind, for some of the same paper stock seems to be present in both manuscripts. A piece of evidence that one would think certainly proves the postmortem date is that the title reads, in English translation, "Concerning Christian Doctrine. Two Posthumous Books Drawn Only from Sacred

Scriptures." Standing as this title does at the beginning of Skinner's transcription, the word translated as "Posthumous" could only postdate November 1674 and antedate the transcription that follows.[26] But such evidence is questionable, because the spacing of the word "posthumi" (also in his hand) indicates that it was a later addition, squeezed into the line it ends. The positioning on page 7 of the original manuscript is

De
Doctrina Christiana

ex sacris duntaxat libris petito
disquisitionum libri duo posthumi
Liber Primus

This spacing suggests that "posthumi" was added some time after the title was completed and, of course, after Milton's death, but it cannot date the transcription of the treatise itself.

Names of its presumed author that certainly were added late to the manuscript also raise vexing questions. It is evident from examination of the original pages of *DDC* that they bore no author's name at all. Instead one can see, because of their positioning with regard to Skinner's original text, that someone has printed "Ioannus Miltonus Anglus" at the top of page 1 before the introductory Epistle, "Ioannis MiltonI Angli" above the title on page 7 (discussed above), and the initials "I.M." on page 5 at the end of the Epistle. All these letters are made with a blunt pen (or heavy hand), quite unlike Skinner's neat calligraphy in the treatise that follows.[27] Skinner's original copy, transcribed from what we presume was Picard's manuscript, evidently had not included these ascriptions.

Because they are printed, final identification of the writer seems impossible. Their purpose, however, is obvious: to identify the author of an otherwise quite anonymous manuscript. Their recognition of Milton as "Englishman" may have been imitated from the same identification prefixed to each of his three *Defenses*. Thomas Burgess had mentioned this possibility in a postscript to his essay discrediting Milton as author of *DDC*.[28] The bookseller Moses Pitt had been associated in some way with Skinner, who seems to have consulted him about publishing his two manuscripts. Pitt may have added this identification of *DDC* (the State Papers were self-identifying), for Burgess pointed out that in 1673 Pitt had named Milton's friend John Selden author of a work actually by Alexander Sardo (by "Ioannis Seldeni Angli") to which he added a fraudulent dedication. Burgess concluded that Skinner's transcription of the treatise with Milton's name added thus to it "seems to have been made for some purpose of disguise,"[29] though both inscriptions could, of course, have been added innocently for identification of the assumed author. Such textual history fails, however, to explain the subscribing of the two letters "I.M." at the end of the Epistle. This addition is difficult to excuse as innocent.

The Two Scribes

Or these three additions may have been supplied after the recovery of the manuscript by Lemon in 1823. It is clear that he felt it necessary to authenticate his discovery because he had his son and a friend swear as witnesses to it.[30] For his edition of the work, he had an engraved copy made of its opening page 7, but on this reproduction there is no Latin ascription to Milton or to anyone else. Gordon Campbell has written me in a private letter that engravers "did not omit names," with the implication that the printed name was added later after the engraver had done his work—after 1823, that is.

Furthermore, Lemon was a good friend, as Campbell has also pointed out to me, of the nefarious John Payne Collier, now recognized as the most skillful forger of documents in English literary history. Campbell adds that Collier is known to have had access to the *DDC* manuscript, and he certainly knew enough about inks to have prepared a suitably early one such as was used for these letters. On the other hand, if Lemon did engage Collier's assistance, it may have been only an innocent identification of a manuscript that one would have expected the forger to have done more skillfully. Yet again, it is difficult to explain innocently the presence of the two initials at the end of the Epistle. Burgess too spotted all these additions[31] but apparently did not question Lemon about them, assuming Pitt's responsibility. What then of the testimony of Lemon's facsimile, which lacked the name and which Burgess surely knew?

In conclusion, the printed names and initials possibly were added in 1675 or 1676 when Skinner was trying to place the manuscript with a publisher. Moses Pitt seems more likely to have made the additions than Skinner who, one would expect, would have matched his own neat handwriting on the rest of these two pages, as "posthumi" does. Or they were added by Lemon and Collier after the recovery of the manuscript in 1823 and after the engraver had made his reproduction of page 7. In any case, the original work carried no express recognition of who had authored it. Finally, to repeat, the evidence of all the early biographers except Phillips traces back to the Anonymous Biography and to Aubrey's "Minutes," which report mostly from a distance Skinner's erroneous, but probably innocent, ascription of the *DDC* manuscript to Milton. Because the latter's relationships with Milton were at best marginal, we simply cannot trust his evidence of who authored the work.

Chapter Four

Canon and Treatise: Similarities and Differences

Those who have examined at all closely volume 6 of the *Complete Prose* must be perplexed that anyone would question Milton's full responsibility for it as author. Maurice Kelley, its able and diligent editor, cited literally hundreds of parallels between its text and those in the acknowledged canon. Such parallels he found from Milton's earliest publications to his latest, but they are especially significant for the works dictated later in his career, when the evidence of Picard's activity supports 1658 to 1660 as the period when volume 6 was written. Thus it coincides with the dictation of *Paradise Lost* and with the actual publication of *Of Civil Power* and *Hirelings*, both 1659, and *Readie and Easie Way*, with two editions in early 1660. How then can anyone confronted with this wealth of evidence that Kelley has produced argue any kind of distance between the treatise and the accepted canon?

Visitation Unimplor'd

In assembling his collection of analogues Kelley was not, in those days, trying to prove that the treatise had originated with Milton, an assumption that no one had challenged since the 1820s. Kelley's useful purpose, rather, was to show how the work could provide valuable insights as a gloss to Milton's other writings. Thus a great many of his notes comparing this text with those of the canon cite similarities to be anticipated between any works dependent on interpretations common to the Reformed understanding of scripture, either in support of or in disagreement with them, without necessarily ascribing to anyone the authorship of the treatise. Indeed, the Bible itself, as one would expect, is the direct source for many of the similarities that Kelley has pointed out.

For an example of a significant verbal likeness, book 1, chapter 10 of the treatise terms the Tree of Knowledge of good and evil in Paradise "a kind of pledge [pignus] or memorial of obedience" (6.352), just as in *Paradise Lost* (3.95) the Tree is "sole pledge of his [Adam's] obedience." The word "pledge," even with only its Latin equivalent, seems to be a real likeness without biblical precedent (but not "obedience," which is commonplace in this context). Perhaps Milton was indeed actively engaged with *this chapter* of the treatise and adopted its word in his poem. Less specifically verbal parallels, however, must be approached with caution. For instance, *DDC* warns its readers against "our being carried beyond the reach of human comprehension, and outside the written authority of scripture, into vague subtleties of speculation," to which Kelley subjoins ten passages from

Paradise Lost (6.133–34 and n. 12). But the point is commonplace, most famously demonstrated in Marlowe's *Dr. Faustus.*

The most recent and prolific proponent of treating parallels between treatise and canon as conclusive proof of single authorship has been Christopher Hill. Because of his well-deserved reputation, some readers may accept without question his assertions, many of which rely, of course, upon such generally accepted concordances as mortalism (the doctrine that the soul dies with the body: *Paradise Lost* 10.782–94 and *DDC*, book 1, chapter 13).[1] Close inspection, however, may reveal significant problems. Hill divided his attack into seven sections plus an extensive appendix—far too long to consider here item by item. It may be instructive to examine in some detail the accuracy of the first part.

Hill begins by identifying T.F. Tout, the author of the biography of Bishop Burgess in the *Dictionary of National Biography*, and giving him his personal seal of approval, with which I certainly agree. After all, I had used the same authority to establish who Burgess was in my report of my recovery of his work, much of which Hill has repeated. But then he goes on to stress what he infers from Tout as Burgess's "dotage" when in 1829 the Bishop published *Milton Not the Author of Milton*. The trouble is that Tout shows no sign of having read it, and Hill could not, for no copy had been located in Britain until Ogden's essay appeared. No one who has read Burgess's rare book could possibly accuse him of being in his dotage when he wrote it. In 1993 I added, after giving the evidence, that "the absence of copies [of the book] needs to be accounted for" and went on to say that "Arguments from silence are inconclusive but can be suggestive"—a statement that Hill quotes, adding that Tout had "explained this silence" as resulting from the Bishop's senility. Clearly I was at fault here, assuming that everyone would reach the conclusion of royal censorship, for which I provided the evidence without spelling out what I thought was obvious.

I thought too that I had made clear how Burgess had supported King George IV against emancipating Roman Catholics in contemporary England and, indeed, had republished *Of True Religion*, with his long Preface distancing Milton from *DDC*, as part of that struggle. Thus he saw the treatise as not so strongly anti-Catholic as Milton usually was. Hill makes this a point of departure for a lecture to theological innocents on the word "Anti-Christ" as applied to the Papacy and, having pointed out that it "occurs only once directly and once indirectly in the treatise (pp. 604, 798)," goes on to assert that the word had been so overused as to make it quite unpopular then (p. 166). If the term had fallen out of favor, no one had bothered to tell Milton about it in the late 1650s, for in *Of Civil Power* he used the word or its derivatives with this Papal application four times (7.244, 245) and again in *Of True Religion* (8.434). Hill's emphasis upon the reluctance of the treatise to employ the word nicely distances it from Milton's willingness to use it in a contemporary text, another small detail to support my distancing of *DDC* from the canon.

Hill next attacks Burgess's argument that "our recent translation" (6.242) of the New Testament—not of the whole Bible, as Hill has it—is that of Felbinger, published in 1660 in Amsterdam, rather than the usually accepted Walton *Polyglot* of 1657. Hill's argument is simplicity itself: Milton knew Walton and helped him import paper for his great work, as indeed is true. Therefore, "The poet is much more likely to have thought of the Polyglot ... than an Arian *New Testament* published in Amsterdam of which there is no reason to suppose that he had ever heard" (167), as indeed there isn't. His argument depends upon an error of elementary logic, that of begging the question: he assumes that Milton is the author in order to prove that he would not have known the Felbinger translation. I shall question Burgess's identification on quite other grounds. These observations bring me to the end of Hill's first section (165–68).

A second example of problems that one may face with uncritical acceptance of Hill's assertions is a single paragraph[2] that lists "Minor points [of agreement between treatise and canon] noted by Kelley [that] include:

1. "the Archangel Michael as leader of the angels"—as indeed he is so described in Revelation 12.7, evidently familiar to both the author of *DDC* and Milton, as to anyone who reads the verse.
2. "Satan's names, his despair, and even his wandering over the earth." Actually Satan gets less than a page (6.349–50) in the treatise. His various names (6.350) do not figure at all in *Paradise Lost*. The evil angels, not

Satan, are the ones who despair in the treatise (not as in the poem), though one may assume that he did too. *DDC* does not distinguish Satan from Beelzebub as the poem does. As for "his wandering over the earth," the source for this activity of both the fallen angels (6.348) and of Satan in *Paradise Lost* is Job 1.7, the first proof text cited here in the treatise. Surely the author of *Paradise Lost* was also familiar with it.

3. "He needed divine permission to leave hell"—else God, of course, is not omnipotent.

4. "That the name of Joshua corresponded to Jesus is noted in both; each led the children of Israel through the wilderness to the land of Canaan"—a connection available to anyone trained in both Hebrew and Greek, for these are the forms of a single name in the respective languages. As the biblical text makes clear, both the human Joshua and "the Lord"—interpreted by Christians as the Son—were salvific agents.

5. "The *DDC*'s heresies are present in *Paradise Lost*, though expressed with an ambiguity too skillful to be accidental. Anti-Trinitarianism, for instance. 'Of all creation first/Begotten Son'—and many other references to the Son as a 'creature.' ('First of created things'—*DDC*, 206)." In a subsequent chapter I shall consider the points he has raised about the Son, and others associated with them. I cannot find in the poem the "many other references to the Son as a 'creature'"; indeed, there are none.

To complete the paragraph, Hill adds a few further references to eccentric ideas that appear in *DDC*—but only in it. Inasmuch as they do not cite any canonic work, he cannot argue a common authorship. He concludes that "Kelley is especially good on the parallel use of proof texts in the two works," a point with which I agree, having elaborated this analytical approach in 1976. I shall considerably expand its applicability in a later chapter. Hill's appendix (188–93) is far too long to respond to in detail. I believe I have considered in one context or another all of its significant points as well as those in the rest of his essay.

Some direct insights derive from close analysis of the similarities between *DDC* and the prose tracts published during the years Milton was supposedly also occupied with it. Such congruities indeed exist, for the treatise dwells in places on the subjects of both *Of Civil Power* and *Hirelings*. The former, centered on the separation of church and state—an issue not finally resolved even today—has at least three parallel statements on this subject that Kelley indexes to volume 6 in the introductory Epistle to the treatise (6.120, 123, and 124); another cluster in book 1, chapter 27 on the Covenant of Grace (6.535, 536, 539 and 541); again in book 1, chapter 30, on the scriptures (6.583, 584, 590, and 592); and finally in book 1, chapter 32, on church discipline (6.607, 611, 612 and 613). Kelley's useful index also notes a few other isolated parallels.

Hirelings takes up a specific facet of the subject discussed in *Of Civil Power*, the tithing tax imposed by governments to support their religious establishments. In *DDC* Kelley notes a cluster of parallels in book 1, chapter 28, on the Covenant of Grace (6.548, 558 and 561), and the most extensive group in book 1, chapter 31 on churches (6.593, 595, 596, 598, 599, 600, 602 and 603), though so large a number is not unexpected in view of the subject of this chapter—support of ministers by tithes.

Finally, Kelley has indexed a few parallels in the treatise to Milton's late *Of True Religion* (1673), but they are scattered—which one might expect from the generalized subject matter of this pamphlet—as compared with the unification of each of the other two around a clearly limited topic. In all such parallels one does not find, nor expect to find, exact verbal duplication, because of the language difference between *DDC* and the three tracts. Certainly there is parallelism of ideas, which sometimes suggests interdependence, possibly common authorship, and sometimes common dependence on another source, often the Bible.

In view of the hundreds of parallels cited in Kelley's notes, it is manifestly impossible to discuss all of them here. Instead I will analyze the most extensive sample, those noted to *Hirelings* in book 1, chapter 31, "Of Particular Churches." The many parallels exist because this is the fullest argument in *DDC* against tithing, the subject also of *Hirelings*. I number the parallels and briefly comment on each. Regrettably, such an approach must involve some tedium.

1. Ministers of churches are presbyters and deacons (6.593, at n. 2), exactly paralleled in *Hirelings* (7.283). The similarity is not significant, however, for this is the standard position of Reformed churches.

2. Some remuneration may properly be paid ministers

(6.595, at n. 4), a point confirmed but not so strongly stated in *Hirelings* (7.280–81) with different proof texts. These texts separate otherwise similar positions.

3. Paul urged himself as an example of an unpaid minister, and if one follows his example one can avoid giving "all offense or suspicion" (6.596, at n. 5), an opinion with which *Hirelings* agrees (7.280) with the realistic addition, "but few such are to be found." Paul was, of course, the model unpaid minister extolled by all anti-tithers, of whom there were thousands in England alone. The example is not sufficiently distinctive to prove any interdependence.

4. Many have argued that "If you take away ecclesiastical revenues, you destroy the gospel" (6.598, at n. 6), which is closely matched in *Hirelings*: "if ye settle not our maintenance by law, farwell the gospel" (7.318). This indeed is a significant parallel suggesting interdependence or common authorship.

5. If Christianity is "based upon and supported by violence and money, why should it be thought more worthy of respect than Mohomedanism?" (6.598), concluding the sentence that begins with item 4. *Hirelings* makes exactly the same comparison: "how can any Christian object it to a Turk, that his religion stands by force only [?]" (7.318). The clear identity of ideas here seems impossible to explain away by postulating a common source; the Moslem references are convincing. A single author then seems to have composed the statements in both texts. Confirmation may be found in the fact that the distinctive ideas in the sentence formed by items 4 and 5 are also found together in both treatise (598) and tract (318), near the end but quite separate from the other parallels Kelley has noted. There is no textual evidence that the ideas are a late intrusion into Picard's manuscript text.[3] Thus one may conclude that Milton wrote both. But another equally valid

explanation exists for these important parallels: Milton found the sentence useful from a reading of the manuscript and used it in his own tract, where it appears perhaps as an afterthought near the conclusion.

6. The interest of ministers in being paid will bring wolves into the church (6.598, at n. 8), an idea which recurs in *Hirelings* (7.280) and elsewhere in Milton's writings, most famously in *Paradise Lost* (12.507–11). But this development from Acts 20.29 is commonplace with every anti-tither. One must notice that the proof texts cited in this passage of *DDC* differ significantly from those cited in *Hirelings*.

7. It is disgraceful for a minister to sue his parishioners for tithes, a practice unknown "in any reformed church except ours" (6.598–99, at n. 9). But Kelley's citation here from *Hirelings* (7.281) is not pertinent. I shall return below to further consideration of the collection of tithes.

8. It is wrong for a minister "to force his instruction upon those who do not want to be taught by him" and "to exact payment" from "a man who rejects you as a teacher and whom you would reject as a pupil if it were not for the money" (6.599, at n. 10), the latter part of the sentence being paralleled in *Hirelings* (7.300–301), where church members are "compelld to recompense the parochial minister, who neither chose him for thir teacher, nor have received instruction from him," with the important addition not present in *DDC*, because he is "insufficient or not resident or inferior to whom they follow." Nonresidency is not an issue anywhere in *DDC*, but it certainly was in mid-century England. Otherwise the ideas may be significantly parallel.

9. Ministers should follow the example of prophets, who chopped wood and built their own houses, of Christ as a carpenter, and of Paul (6.600, at n. 12). Kelley's long note

to *Hirelings* (7.305-6) cites the well-worn example of Paul, but then goes on to the similar but not at all pertinent subject of the self-sufficiency of the Waldensians. It is important to note that they are never mentioned anywhere in *DDC* but are a major subject in *Hirelings*.[4]

10. Unlike Paul, ministers contend that they should be repaid for their education "from the proceeds of the gospel" (6.600, at n. 13). Likewise in *Hirelings* (7.314) ministers claim that their education has been "very chargeable" and so they should be repaid by "a plentiful maintenance," an argument which is indeed close to the claims attacked in *DDC*.

11. "The synagogue was a particular assembly... but it was not a particular church, because the total and entire worship of God could not properly be performed in the synagogue" (6.602, at n. 16), to which *Hirelings* parallels "tithes were fitted to the *Jewes* only, a national church of many incomplete synagogues; uniting the accomplishment of divine worship in one temple...; but the Christian church is universal; not ti'd to nation, dioces or parish, but consisting of many particular churches complete in themselves" (7.292). Similarities are indeed present here, but the two texts read like the thesis of some other author defining the differences between synagogues and churches. The *DDC* statement omits the reason the Jewish practices were important: tithing is a legal requirement only in the Old Testament.

12. Continuing the contrast of synagogue and church, at the time of the book of Acts, the treatise affirms, there was "only one national universal Jewish church, and no particular churches. But now there is no national church and a great number of particular churches, each absolute in itself" (6.602, at n. 17). As a parallel Kelley cites *Hirelings* (7.308), and one should add the parallel of item 11 about

the individuality of Christian congregations. Both statements come from a convinced congregationalist.

Shortly thereafter chapter 31 ends. There certainly are parallels between tract and treatise; one, the Moslem allusions, seems to me to prove some kind of interaction. Others are less persuasive, the arguments of anti-tithers anywhere. The total absence from *DDC* of any mention of the Waldensians, for whom Milton was deeply concerned after their "massacre" in 1655, suggests some distance between the two works. One other difference also must be recognized: the arguments in treatise and tract do not parallel each other at all in the order in which issues are presented. Some may conclude common authorship; but I believe that Milton found useful at least one detail, the Moslem comparison, and perhaps others that he adapted to his own argument. Such use of material does not prove him author of the chapter, which I believe predated his tractates of 1659.

I now turn to fundamental discrepancies between *Hirelings* and *DDC*.

1. One to be considered in the discussion of proof texts is the total avoidance in *DDC* of any mention of Melchizedek as a compelling model for tithing in the tract (7.284–90 and 297). Likewise missing is even the slightest allusion to the important arguments of Henry Spelman and William Prynne, which bulk large throughout *Hirelings*. Barbara Lewalski would explain this as owing to the fact that *DDC* is narrowly addressed to a Continental audience,[5] a fact with which I agree; but she avoids any consideration of why Milton as its author should so totally dissociate himself from his own people. As noted above,

there is no mention of the Waldensians in *DDC*. Its author evidently did not know, as Milton did, his friend John Selden's *History of Tithes* (1618), which would have been very useful, as it was for *Hirelings*, nor his *Uxor Hebraea* (1646), which Milton also cites by name (7.299).

2. One section of Milton's attack on tithing equated the "greedy" priesthood with the sons of Eli—that is, with the sons of Belial (7.296; 1 Samuel 2.12). He also used this material in a somewhat different sense in *Paradise Lost* I, 490ff. This vivid allusion finds no place anywhere in *DDC*.

3. The legal procedures for collecting tithes recounted in *DDC* were not those used in England, as Bishop Burgess pointed out long ago: in historical fact the argument "is inapplicable to England or Holland."[6] The treatise makes the ministers themselves responsible:

> To bargain for or exact tithes or gospel-taxes, to extort a subsidy from the flock by force or by the intervention of the magistrates, to invoke the civil law in order to secure church revenue and to take such matters into the courts—these are the actions of wolves, not ministers of the gospel. . . . How disgraceful is it, then, for a man of the church to enter into litigation with his flock . . . for the sake of tithes, which are the property of others. This sort of thing does not go on in any reformed church except ours (6.598–99).

In *Hirelings* Milton never mentions this practice, because it was not the procedure he knew in England. What he does write is that English supporters of forced tithing (he has primarily in mind Spelman and Prynne) claim it "under the gospel" as well as "under the law"—a claim made only by "our English divines and they only of all Protestants" (7.281). The author of *DDC* is quite unaware of this exceptional English claim, which was not made on the Continent.[7] In England, laymen called "impropriators" collected tithes; as a speculative investment people paid for this privilege in specific parishes. The most famous such lay impropriator was William Shakespeare, who in July 1605 invested £440 for half-interest in the lease of "Tythes of Corne, grayne blade & haye" in three villages near Stratford.[8] English priests did not sue their parishioners for support as the treatise reports them doing.

4. The treatise devotes a single sentence to the history of tithing, which "originated either in the spoils of war, or in the voluntary vow of some individual, or in that agrarian law [of the Old Testament] which was not only abrogated long ago but which never had any thing to do with us anyway" (6.599). Milton's knowledge of this history is much more comprehensive. In *Hirelings* he recognizes the requirement of tithing in the Mosaic law, which he can easily discard because for Christians it is ceremonial rather than moral and thus of no effect (a distinction that I shall consider at length below). The author of *DDC* knew this too. Then Milton spends pages discounting the model of Melchizedek, which *DDC* downplays merely as "the spoils of war." He next traces the history of English tithing practices from Saxon laws and "*Peters* penny" that was paid to

the Pope (7.294). The author of *DDC* ignores all this. One may excuse him on the grounds that he was narrowly limiting his audience to the Continent, though again there is no clear reason for its author to have done so. Anyone with Milton's erudition on this subject would have been unlikely to be satisfied with the single sentence of the history of tithes quoted here from *DDC*.

One expects agreement on many details between Milton's works and *DDC* because they share the common heritage of Reformed Protestantism. An obvious example is the fact that both postulate two classes of church officers, elders and deacons. My concern is for the doctrinal relationships between *DDC* and the canonic works—sometimes in direct contradiction, sometimes in modification of views held by the other, sometimes arguing positions that the other ignores. For instance, they fundamentally disagree on the relative significance of scripture and of accompanying spiritual revelation. In view of his extraordinarily heavy reliance upon biblical texts, it is disconcerting that the author of the treatise downplays scriptural authority in favor of the illumination that the "Spirit" can provide. He recognizes the primacy of scripture for one's early religious experiences, but in one's maturity "the pre-eminent and supreme authority" is that of "the Spirit, which is internal, and the individual possession of each man" (6.587). Furthermore, the biblical text may not be reliable: because of faulty transmission, that of the New Testament "is, in fact, corrupt . . . but no one can corrupt the Spirit" (6.587–88). He judges the Old Testament text to be more accurate. For him, spiritual enlightenment evidently far outweighs textual.

Clearly the author here is remembering his own experience as a boy ("adolescens") under Milton's tutelage when he collected extensive biblical texts to prove Wolleb's or Ames's dogmas. Later as an adult the "Spirit" rather than the "letter" revealed new religious truths to him which again he fitted out with textual proofs but not the massed collections of his earlier days. These "Spiritual" revelations account for the many religious eccentricities that mark his later but not his earlier thinking. Such reliance upon the "Spirit" was widely deplored by the orthodox in those days as resulting from "enthusiasm"—by etymology, "possession by God"—which they stoutly resisted because of the heresies it might support, as *DDC* eloquently proves.

To the contrary, Milton recognized with other Protestants that religious truth derives from interpreting scripture as the Holy Spirit directs but without asserting the "pre-eminent and supreme authority" of the latter. In *Of Civil Power* he wrote that "the main foundation of our protestant religion . . . [has] no other divine rule or autoritie from without us . . . as a common ground but the holy scripture, and no other within us but the illumination of the Holy Spirit so interpreting that scripture." He finds no differences in the accuracy of the two Testaments. The printed word cannot "be understood without this divine illumination," but one may not know this illuminating Spirit "at all times to be in himself" (7.242). Like the author of the treatise, Milton thus finds religious truth in the study of scripture under spiritual guidance; but unlike him, he does not question the general truth of the former, whereas he acknowledges that at times the latter may fail. For the author of *DDC* the exact reverse is true: possible failure of religious insights lies in textual corruption, not in the unfailing leadership of the Spirit. This position is very close to that of the Quakers, with whom Milton had ties, but these connections seem more social than doctrinal.

An important and to some a persuasive parallel between canon and treatise is their similar understanding of the obedience to Old Testament law by Christians. At the end of *Of Civil Power*, having devoted the entire tract to denying the Erastian position that the state has an obligation to intervene in religious issues, Milton concludes that the magistrate's sole function in this respect is "the defense only of the church." As for the Ten Commandments, they do not provide any authority for such intervention—either in religious issues (the first four, or the "first table") or in civil ones (the last six, or the "second table") although civil authorities claim such power from them (7.271).

At issue is the distinction recognized between the "ceremonial" and the "moral" laws of the Old Testament. Normative Protestantism viewed the former as applying only to Jews, the latter to all mankind. The food laws and tithing are examples of the ceremonial, the Ten Commandments of the moral. As he concludes *Of Civil Power*, Milton asserts that civil crimes are not crimes "against the second table," as exemplified by coveting (the Tenth Commandment). And indeed it is not a civil crime to covet anything. "What power they [the Commandments] have," he continues, "they had from the beginning." They are, that is, universal laws for all mankind, not just for Jews. Whether binding on all mankind or whether they should "be kept by any Christian," he concludes, "remanes yet as undecided, as it is sure they never were yet deliverd to the keeping of any Christian magistrate"—the last being Milton's main point, not the denial of their authority for believers.

The treatise devotes several pages (6.525–36) to this "undecided" subject, the authority for Christians of the Ten Commandments. What Milton tentatively considered, its author strongly affirms; for the treatise asserts that "all the old covenant, in other words the entire Mosaic law, is abolished . . .; we are released from the decalogue too" (6.525–26). Two solid pages of biblical quotations support this extreme position, words that their author thinks everyone else has "taken to refer to the abolition of the *ceremonial* code only"; whereas he applies them to the *moral* as well (6.528. Here and subsequently I italicize *ceremonial* and *moral* so as to call attention to their specialized meanings). The treatise declares that the "principal reasons [that others have] given for the enactment of the law as a whole, are . . . to stimulate our depravity, and thus cause anger; to inspire us with slavish fear . . .; to be a schoolmaster to bring us to the righteousness of Christ, and so on." In contrast, its author thinks that the texts he quotes prove that for the righteous "every one of these reasons has now been removed" (6.528).

The spiritual issue that any religious legalist faced was the danger that, by keeping the laws, a Christian could by such "works" earn his salvation, so to speak; the Pauline affirmation of salvation by faith would be ignored. All Protestants would recognize the problem, but not many would consequently do away with the whole *moral* law. Like those to whom *DDC* is responding, the Protestants kept it as a tactic to frighten sinners into recognition of the salvation offered in the New Testament. Thus the *Westminster Confession* (19.5, 6) asserts that "the *moral* law doth forever bind all . . . to the obedience thereof" though not "as a covenant of works." Yet it goes on, like the unnamed opponents of the treatise, such laws are "of great use to them [by] discovering also the sinful pollutions of their nature . . . together with a clearer sight of the need they have of Christ." It can also for the regenerate "restrain their corruption . . .; and the threatenings of it serve to show whatever their sins deserve."

In contrast with the position of *DDC*, which rejects this reason to retain the moral laws, but akin to that of the *Confession*, which does retain them with this modified significance, Michael in *Paradise Lost* tells Adam that biblical laws will continue to be significant to mankind

> to evince
> Thir natural pravity, by stirring up

> Sin against Law to fight; that when they see
> Law can discover sin . . .
> they may conclude
> Some bloud more precious must be paid for Man
> . . . which the law by *Ceremonies*
> Cannot appease, nor than the *moral* part
> Perform. (12.287–99)

In this indirect way law can lead from "works of Law to works of Faith" (12.306), just the position that *DDC* opposes in its argument that all Old Testament laws have been abrogated because they are no longer necessary for the regenerate.

One specific regulation that Milton had to counter in both *Of Civil Power* and *Hirelings*, though for very different reasons, was that derived from the Fourth Commandment, observance of the Sabbath. He had to consider the issue in the former work because Erastian regulations of such worship would limit religious freedom, and in the latter because the supporters of tithing had applied its authority in analogous support for their position.

In *Of Civil Power* Milton inveighs against a Parliamentary act governing the Lord's Day that had been passed on 26 June 1657. "Christian liberty," he asserts, "sets us free not only from the bondage of those *ceremonies*, but also from the forcible imposition [by civil law] of those circumstances [for observing them; that is, legislating the] place and time in worship of God" (7.262; emphasis and additions mine). Thus "the best and learnedest reformed writers" support "our freedom not only from *ceremonies* but from those circumstances also [of legally defined place and time], though impos'd with a confident persuasion of *moralitie* in them." He goes on to point out that "the best and most reformed churches abroad" do not support such civil regulations (7.263).

The author of *DDC* can treat this issue much more generally in view of his argument that *all* Old Testament laws are abrogated for Christians and with them the Sabbath itself. It is obvious that he has no Erastian opponents: his Continental audience did not attempt to make such legal regulations of the ceremony as troubled Milton. Indeed, the author of *DDC* needs to give only a single sentence to the problem of such civil control: "there must be no question of its being enforced by the civil authority" (6.714). In contrast, the issue was fundamental throughout Milton's tract.

Hirelings confronts the interpretation of the Fourth Commandment quite differently. In order to require statutory tithing, "our new reformed Presbyterian divines," Milton asserts, want to "impose on us a Judaical *ceremonial* law" as such laws had been understood (7.295), arguing "that tithes may be *moral* as well as the sabbath, a tenth of fruits as well as a seaventh of dayes." As one gave a seventh of his time, he must also give a tenth of his income. Milton answers to the contrary that by thus "denying *morality* in the sabbath"—denying the force of the Fourth Commandment by making it analogous to the *ceremonial* law of tithing—"the seaventh day is not *moral*, but a convenient recourse of worship in fit season, whether seaventh or other number" (7.295). He asserts, as he had in *Of Civil Power*, that such "denying [of] *morality* in the sabbath" is "better agreeing with reformed churches abroad than the rest of our divines." An interesting possibility is that Milton learned about Continental practices directly from the author of *DDC* who, as has been shown, was responding to issues there with which he was well acquainted, though the definition of Sabbatarianism was not one of them. The definition in *Hirelings* of the Lord's Day as "a convenient recourse of worship in fit season, whether seaventh or other number" is analogous to the position expressed in *DDC*: it is "a day of voluntary observance" that "may conveniently recur every seven days, and particularly as the first day of every week" (6.714). But *DDC* does not attribute this position to "the allegations of a divine command, borrowed from the decalogue" (6.714). In conclusion, Milton and the person responsible for the treatise agree in some respects upon the lack of authority of Old Testament law for Christians, but they approach the subject from quite different positions, and the latter adopts a more extreme stand.

Chapter Five

The Continental Context

Two of the most difficult objections to overcome if *DDC* is to be ascribed to Milton are its orientation to Continental authorities and its concomitant disregard of English ones. These are especially troublesome facts to explain if it indeed originated with "John Milton, Englishman," as its added caption asserts twice. In his challenge to the authenticity of the treatise as Milton's this was one of the strongest objections made by Bishop Burgess.[1]

The absence of such references is made even more complete when one recognizes that the single certainly English citation, that of John Selden's *Uxor Hebraea* of 1646, occurs in a passage added to an already completed chapter. It is difficult to imagine an Englishman supporting any religious position that he invites his fellow countrymen to take seriously without a single mention, for his Anglican audience, of the Thirty-Nine Articles and their *Constitutions and*

Canons of 1640 (to which Milton had taken vigorous exception), and, for Presbyterians and some Independents, the *Westminster Confession of Faith*. After all, the latter condemned Milton publicly (though not by name) in its denunciation of "Divorcers" in 1647.[2] The author of *DDC*, on the other hand, shows no reluctance in citing the *Acta et Scripta* (1620) of the Continental Synod of Dort (probably 6.176 and 185, and by name 512). I cannot think of a reason for an English author to focus his attention so resolutely upon non-English authorities. Why should a work addressed, as its opening sentence promises, "To All the Churches of Christ and all in any part of the world who profess the Christian Faith," so absolutely exclude compatriots whose work Milton certainly knew and in some cases had publicly disagreed with? I fail to find any motive in his later years for such a narrowing of interest. The limited outlook of *DDC* can easily be explained as that of a Continental author—or one trained there—addressing an audience indifferent to religious debates across the Channel.

Then or now any discussion of religious issues in England could not be mounted without some consideration of Richard Hooker's *Laws of Ecclesiastical Polity*. A recent, authoritative study by Paul Stanwood of the relationships between Milton's antiprelatical pamphlets and Hooker's *Laws* observes correctly that this "greatest of Anglican theologians and apologists" wields "an influence impossible to ignore."[3] But the author of *DDC* found it quite possible, for he never named or quoted him. Kelley's full index, which includes all the works cited to illuminate the treatise, does not have a single entry for the *Laws*. Stanwood is able to point out parallels in the treatise on a few topics—"the marks of the visible church," that only Christ can be its head, that an individual may constitute himself a church if none is conveniently at hand, that the Scriptures are clear to believers as the written word interpreted as one is inspired by the Holy Spirit, and so on (78–79). But on all these issues the several variations of Protestantism essentially agree. Stanwood can claim no narrowly specific parallels in *DDC*. To the contrary, Hooker is cited in the canonical works once by name in *Church Government* (1.759), and Stanwood draws together a number of other specific issues in which the *Laws* and the canonical works are congruent.

Equally surprising, as Bishop Burgess observed, is the absence of any other of England's active theologians—the Cambridge fellow, Joseph Mede; the still-remembered Anglicans Henry Hammond (1605–60) and Jeremy Taylor (1613–67) and others;[4] or such Calvinists as William Perkins (1558–1602) and the controversialist William Prynne (1600–69). None of them receives the slightest mention in *DDC*. In book 1, chapter 5, on the Son of God, one expects vainly to find at least a remote allusion to the most famous of the contemporary English Unitarians, John Bidle. The treatise does, however, rely upon the very popular *Medulla Theologiae* (1623 and later) of William Ames (1576–1633), who was indeed an Englishman and former fellow at Milton's college at Cambridge, Christ's, until he was driven away because of his strongly Calvinistic beliefs. Early in the century he established himself in Holland, and, until his death there, he was intimately related by both his teaching and his publications to that country. Burgess observed that he clearly identified himself with Holland in another of his books, the *Coronis ad Collationem Hagiensem*, where Ames refers to several Dutch authorities as "our [nostri] divines." The "oppositi" who were his opponents were "the Remonstrant Divines" there.[5]

Once, however, the treatise, in referring to the *Medulla*, titles its author "our countryman Ames" (6.706)—proof, some have thought, that the author of *DDC* was English, as Ames had been by birth and education. Indeed, one must consider seriously the several references made by the author of the treatise to "our" authorities as a means of identifying his theological and geographical orientation. In the case of Ames, it seems more likely that *DDC*'s author was writing as an admirer of a fellow theologian who had identified himself with Holland, as Burgess argued.

Paul Sellin has brought to my attention a similar identification made by a Dutch author with impeccable identification there, Gisbertus Voetius of Utrecht. In his *Politicae Ecclesiasticae* (Amsterdam, 1666), he praises the exceptions to the idea that marriage is indissoluble taken by "our [nostrorum]" theologians against the arguments of the Roman Catholic Cardinal Bellarmine. The latter, he writes, had been adequately answered by "ours [nostris]," who include three sturdy Calvinists of the Continent, Molineus, Rivet, and Ames:

The Continental Context

> Exceptiones *Bellarmini* contra argumentum nostrorum ex *Math.* 5. & 19. ut & objectiones pro indissolubili Conjugii vinculo in casu adulterii à nostris satis superque refutatae sunt; nominatim à *Molineo in dispp. Sedanensibus, & Riveto in commentar. ad Hos. 2 v. 2 & Amesio in Bellarm. enervato* (173).
>
> Bellarmine's exceptions to the arguments of our divines from Matthew 5 and 19 as to objections to the indissoluble bond of marriage in the case of adultery have been sufficiently answered above by our divines—namely by Molineus, Rivet, and Ames [with citation of their respective works].

Like Voetius, the author of *DDC*, if he identified with the Low Countries, could claim Ames as "ours" but not necessarily because he himself was English.

Another connection between *DDC*'s author and England has been claimed from a reference to an interpretation of Acts 20.28 in "our recent translation": "The Syriac version [of this verse] reads *Church of Christ* for *Church of God*: similarly our recent translation has *the Church of the Lord*" (6.242). The only truly "recent translation" in England was, of course, the Authorized Version of 1611, but it reads "Church of God." Since H.J. Todd in 1826 (he was countering Burgess's refusal to identify Milton with the newly discovered treatise), "our recent translation" has been thought to be that printed in Brian Walton's *Biblia Sacra Polyglotta* (London, 1657), which has both the Syriac and its Latin translation with this second meaning.[6] Milton was certainly aware of this publication, because he helped arrange for paper used in its printing,[7] and Harris Fletcher has pointed out how readily "Milton" as author of *DDC* could adapt the Latin of the *Polyglot* to his own "Arian" purposes and recognize it as "our recent translation."[8] The word used in this biblical text, that is, is important to the author of *DDC* as he argues his irregular understanding of the Trinity.

To counter this identification of "our recent translation" as the English *Polyglot* of 1657, Bishop Burgess produced a German translation by Jeremias Felbinger published in 1660.[9] It has the same eccentric interpretation of the Son found in the *Polyglot* and probably derives from a comment by Étienne Courcelles, a leading figure in the Remonstrant Seminary in Amsterdam. But the Bishop's argument is somewhat vitiated by the facts that the translation is into German, not the Latin that the treatise cites; it is not associated with a Syriac version; and, while indeed "recent," it is somewhat too recent in 1660 for a work that by all accounts was already well underway.

As the sentence quoted from *DDC* shows, its author pairs the Latin of the New Testament with a version of it in Syriac. But this pairing, repeated in the *Polyglot*, refers in *DDC* not to the *Polyglot* but to Walton's own source for the texts, which also paired the two: *Novum Domini nostri Jesu Christi Testamentum* Syriacé. *Cum Versione Latina* (Anhalt, 1621). Martin Trost, a professor at Wittenberg, had newly edited the former; it was printed with the venerable Latin translation of John Tremellius. Both the Syriac and Latin texts of the latter had appeared in 1569, but

Walton followed the updated 1621 edition which was, of course, available on the Continent. An author there would naturally refer to it as "our recent translation"—"our" again meaning loosely "Protestant." Milton was familiar with the book as was anyone who wanted, before 1657, to cite the currently accepted Syriac text of the New Testament (*Tetrachordon*, 2.647).

Another British author or publication mentioned in the treatise is John Cameron, originally from Scotland; though it cites him by name, the *DDC* does not recognize him as "ours." He lived during all his active years on the Continent and was particularly identified with the Huguenot group at Saumur. There he published in 1626–28 his *Praelectionum in Selectiora loca Novi Testamenti* to which *DDC* may refer (6.534). That Milton himself knew at least one work by this author is clear from references to his *Myrothecium Evangelicum* (Geneva, 1632) five times in *Tetrachordon* (2.647, 656, 660, 684, 687). There is no evidence, however, in any of these references to identify the Milton who cites them with the author of *DDC*.

Another allusion in *DDC* to "our" theologians appears in its analysis of the relationship between faith and works. In the chapter on Justification its author raises

> a question over which there is very fierce controversy: does faith alone justify? *Our* theologians say yes; and hold, moreover, that works are the effects of faith, not the causes of justification. . . . *Others* contend that we

are not justified by faith alone, and they base their argument [for works too] on James ii.24.... As the two points of view seem incompatible, *our* theologians argue that James must be talking about justification [by works] in the sight of men, not in the sight of God. (6.489, emphasis added)

Burgess pointed out that this was not the sense adopted by any of "our" English theologians—Jewell, Hooker, Jackson, Mede, Taylor and Hammond—"who may be considered as the standards of the Church of England doctrine." Rather, the *nostri theologi* of the text, he judged, should "be understood of those of Holland,"[10] though he could not provide any more specific identification.

To choose between Paul's faith that alone justifies before God and James's faith coupled with works, "our theologians" in the foregoing quotation singled out the Pauline. Then, constrained to bring the verse from James about works somehow into harmony with it, they concluded "that James must be talking about justification in the sight of man, not of God," a position that the treatise goes on to reject in the paragraph that follows. In his note quoting an analogue of the sentence, Kelley has shown that this reading of "our theologians" is again that of the Remonstrant Courcelles of Amsterdam (*Opera*, p. 794), who had interpreted James 2.24 in almost identical language: "ilium de justificatione coram Deo non agere, sed de justificatione coram hominibus." The Latin of the treatise reads, "de justificatione coram hominibus non coram Deo" (6.489, n. 6).

The Continental Context

DDC's author goes on to state regretfully that he "cannot imagine what came into our theologians' heads" to lead them to this conclusion (6.490). His own position is that works are necessary too, that true faith inspires them. Arguing from Romans 3.28 "that man is justified by faith without the works of the law," he concludes that Paul has eliminated only works done to fulfill the law, not works that result from faith: "Faith has its own works," and thus "the only living faith is a faith which acts" (6.490). Again Kelley is helpful in establishing the contemporary context of this idea. A follower of Courcelles in Amsterdam, Philip van Limborch (1633–1712), took up the same subject: "When we say we are justified by Faith," he wrote,

> "we do not exclude those Works which Faith requires and produces, since they are included in such a Faith"; and again, "here 'tis objected, that St. Paul in his Epistles to the Romans and the Galatians does all along maintain, that a Man is justified by Faith only, without the Works of the Law. Answ. 'Tis here to be remembered, the apostle does not exclude all Works, but only those of the Law, as he expressly calls them (6.490, n. 7).

The author of *DDC* agrees, though Limborch's position was not yet published when he wrote this.

In sharp contrast with the failure of the treatise to show any awareness of religious thought in England, there is plenty to demonstrate reliance upon writers on the Continent. Inherent in this distancing is the immense gulf between the authorities that Milton cited in his own earlier writings and those that the author of *DDC* found valuable. Had Milton been responsible for it, he totally ignored for the most part the authors upon whom he had relied. In a long note, Kelley has summarized the great disparity between those cited in *DDC* and those in Milton's own publications. Such evidence warrants quotation at some length:

> the *Christian Doctrine* shows little connection with Milton's considerable reading in Renaissance theology for the anti-episcopal and divorce tracts. In these 1641–1645 pamphlets Milton refers to some forty-two works, which may be roughly classified as systematic theologies (by Chamierus, Gerhardus, Peter Martyr, and Melanchthon), treatises on disputed heads of faith (by Arminius, Beza, Bidenbachius, Bucer, Erasmus, Hemingius, Perkins, Rivetus, Salmasius, and Spanheim), and commentaries and exegetical works (by Aretius, Beza, Bucer, Calvin, Cameron, Diodati, Erasmus, Fagius, Grotius, Gualtherius, Hunnius, Peter Martyr, Musculus, Paraeus, and Rivetus). The *Christian Doctrine*, however, mentions none of the systematic theologies or treatises on disputed heads of faith, and with three exceptions makes but minor use of the commentaries and exegetical works.... The three exceptions are Beza, Erasmus, and Junius, whose commentaries Milton makes spare use of in the 1641–1645 prose tracts but employs frequently in the *Christian Doctrine*, while conversely Milton's favorite commentators in the 1641–1645 tracts, Fagius, Grotius, and Paraeus, are not mentioned in the *Christian Doctrine*. (6.22, n. 25)

The Continental Context

A glance at Kelley's list raises what seems to be a troubling question: among the "treatises on disputed heads of faith . . ., commentaries and exegetical works" that he cites as written by authors named by Milton in the 1641 pamphlets, only William Perkins was English. With so little need to rely upon English authorities, it may seem that Milton could indeed be identified with the author of *DDC*, who also needed them seldom or, more accurately, never. Milton indeed cites works by Perkins five times in the two editions of *Doctrine and Discipline*, but he also names many other influential English divines—for example, Launcelot Andrews five times in *Church Government*, Hooker and Tyndale once each, and on numerous occasions the authoritative *Constitutions and Canons* (1640) governing the polity of the Church of England. One should also mention his citation of John Selden twice on legal matters in these pamphlets. Indeed, it would be foolhardy to attack the English bishopric or to favor divorce without thorough grounding in all the major English authorities. On the other hand, as Kelley's note observes correctly, whoever was responsible for *DDC* knew of none of these important English writers, though works like Selden's *De Deis Syriis* could have been of great value to him. (I shall later put into proper perspective the single citation of Selden's *Uxor Hebraea* in book 1, chapter 10.) To name Perkins as the only English divine who was influential on Milton's thought in these works thus gives a distorted view. At the same time, one must not fail to recognize Kelley's main point: how "little connection" the authorities cited in the treatise of the

1650s have with those used by supposedly the same author of the previous decade.

A second of Kelley's always useful notes identifies a number of Reformation theologians or their works upon which *DDC* relies (6.107, n. 34). From his list he removes Bucer, Calvin, Gomarus, Peter Martyr, Musculus and Ursinus as all probably having been cited only at second hand from Andrew Rivet. In order to limit the names to those writers in the Reformed tradition, I also omit here, from his compilation of influential sources, Luther and the Racovian Catechism, along with the politicized *Acta* of the Synod of Dort. There remain William Ames of Franeker, Holland (1576–1633); Theodore Beza, primarily of Geneva (1519–1605); John Cameron (1579?–1625), Louis Cappel or Capell (the name is variously spelled, 1585–1658), and Joshué de La Place (Placaeus, 1604–65), all of Saumur, France; Francis Junius of Heidelberg, then Leiden (1545–1602) and Jerome Zanchi, also of Heidelberg, later Neustadt (1516–1590), Amandus Polanus (1561–1610) and John Wolleb (1586–1629), both of Basel; and Andrew Rivet of Leiden (1572–1651). Not a single one of these authors in his maturity has any significant association with England. Milton, of course, knew and used the ideas of some of them. He cited Cameron seven times in *Tetrachordon* and Rivet on five occasions in *Doctrine and Discipline.* He also quoted the latter several times in his *Commonplace Book*; one of these entries was in the hand of Jeremie Picard, the primary copyist of *DDC* (1.466, n. 10). The ideas of Beza are important for both treatise and canon, as are

The Continental Context

those of Junius: they are primarily responsible for the biblical texts underlying all the discussions. In contrast, the strongly differing treatments of Calvin in the treatise and the canon are significant: the former ignores him, the latter names and refers early and late to his books. But probably the most striking differences of citations are those of the two primary authorities of the treatise, Ames and Wolleb, plus Polanus, a third strongly influential name. Milton himself mentions the first only once (2.610), and Wolleb and Polanus never. Even if we accept that he saw both the former as authors of elementary outlines (as has been shown), one would expect anyone who relied so heavily on both in his theological treatise to allude to them at least occasionally in his other works. Finally, the remaining writers whose influence Kelley finds in *DDC*—Cappel, La Place and Zanchi—like Wolleb and Polanus have no influence whatsoever anywhere on Milton's thought. Two different authors of quite different training must be responsible for treatise and canon.

It may be significant that some major centers of Reformed thinking in the seventeenth century escape attention in *DDC*, like Paris, where Grotius was located, and Geneva, home in mid-century to Spanheim, Turretini, and Milton's enemy More. In striking contrast is the prominence of Basel and especially of Saumur—the latter having earlier been led by Cameron and later by La Place and Cappel (who posed the most important set of proof texts to which *DDC* responds in its arguments about the Son of God). Against La Place's *Disputationes de testimoniis*

(Saumur, 1651), as J.P. Pittion has demonstrated, "Milton" as author of chapter 5 of *DDC* "consciously uses Socinian arguments to defend well-defined Socinian positions" in opposition to its clearly orthodox stand.[11]

It may be significant that, with the widespread affirmation of the Trinity the period afforded, the author of *DDC* chose La Place to attack because of a personal and direct connection with the school at Saumur. A significant fact, too, is that the *Disputationes* seems to be the latest publication—1651—to which the treatise refers, which narrows somewhat the time when it was actively composed. All those works postdating 1651 that Kelley and others have cited as influencing ideas in *DDC* had seen earlier printings. As Pittion confirms, this fact places at least the composition of chapter 5, which disputes the *Disputationes*, after this date, though if *DDC*'s author had been a student at Saumur, he could be responding to lectures that he had earlier attended there. His references to the *Disputationes* are not exact quotations, though they are very close to its meanings.[12]

Although the author of *DDC* thus shows some identification with the school at Saumur in his attacks upon La Place's ideas, he is strangely silent on what is recognized today as Cappel's major achievement there, his proof that vowel points had not been included in the original Old Testament Hebrew texts but had been added much later by scribes. Cappel had published his theory anonymously as early as 1624 in his *Arcanum punctationis revelatum* and repeated it in his *Critica sacra* of 1650.¹³ Evidently the author of *DDC* was not in the least interested in this major textual discovery, for he never mentions it (nor, for that matter, does Milton). The reason for such indifference may be, if he were indeed associated as a student with Saumur around 1650, that Cappel's idea had been totally rejected by most religious leaders—the widely celebrated Buxtorfs of Basel, for example.

Another fact seems to weigh somewhat against identifying the author of *DDC* with Saumur about 1650. During the period of this presumptive association, three theologians shared prominence there: Cappel and La Place, both of whose works he evidently knew, and Moyse Amyraut. The latter, who was also very prominent, receives no mention at all, a fact that I find difficult to account for. If the author of *DDC* was, however, a former student of Milton, as I have suggested, he would have avoided the Salmurian as a bitter opponent of his former teacher. For Amyraut "was scandalized by the beheading of Charles I," and at just this time in 1650 published in Paris a "bitter denunciation of the regicide" entitled *Discours sur la souveraineté des rois*.¹⁴ He was also currently involved in a rancorous redefinition of predestination against charges of heresy, brought against him by Rivet in Holland. The dispute threatened to split apart French Protestantism.¹⁵ But the reasons for *DDC*'s author having distanced himself from Amyraut—if he indeed were associated with him in Saumur around 1650—otherwise remain obscure. The school there "drew numerous students from Geneva, and from the four Swiss cities Basel, Bern,

Schaffhausen, and Zurich."[16] One can surely add some from England. For example, Richard Jones, a former student of Milton's, went there to study in the summer of 1657, evidently with his old teacher's approval. (See the correspondence in 7.487–89, 498–90, and 502–05.)

Besides Saumur, the other contemporary center on the Continent in which the author of *DDC* seems likely to have studied was Holland, where both Socinianism and Arminianism were hotly debated. There in Leidan was one of the most important Reformed authorities of the day, Andrew Rivet, whom he could have known, for Rivet lived until 1651. His thought was certainly influential for the author of the treatise, as it was for Milton. Another theologian important in this area was Courcelles, head of the Remonstrant Academy in Amsterdam.[17] Of the several active Reformed centers on the Continent to which the treatise is responsive, those in Holland and Saumur seem to be the ones in which the author of *DDC* found residency most profitable. To repeat, of the influential names on Kelley's list, all are Continental scholars; none is English. Of them Milton himself drew significantly only upon Beza, Cameron, and Rivet. My conclusion is that, given their responses to such different groups of authorities, we are witnessing the theological backgrounds of two quite different authors.

Chapter Six

Proof from Proof Texts

In order to demonstrate the truth of any detail of their religious positions, members of the Reformed churches copiously quoted verses from the Bible, trusting it alone as the inspired and infallible word of God. Barbara Lewalski has argued this is a characteristic that helps to prove that Milton authored *DDC* inasmuch as both he and it base their positions on "the uses of open discussion . . ., the method of turning first to scripture in doctrinal matters, and only then to authorities . . ., [and] finally, the habit of appealing to scripture and reason together, as harmonious supports for all sorts of arguments."[1] While I agree with all these observations, they are typical of Reformed thought and so are not distinctive enough to prove a single author. Wolleb, for example, in the "Prolegomena" to his *Compendium* asserts that there is "no other basis for theology than the written word of God" and goes on to list "the means of finding out the true meaning of Scripture" as, among others, "logical analysis."² The widely shared acceptance of Ramist dialectic must also discount the coupling of reason with Scripture as a unique characteristic of one author. As the editor-translator of Ames's *Medulla* observes, his "practical advice to his readers is to study the Scripture as good Ramists."³

But various individuals and groups found their truths in various passages from Scripture. By comparing the proof texts used by each, one can recognize a continuity of religious tradition or divergences from it.⁴ *DDC* is noteworthy for its enormous collection of such quotations. By its citation of those used by others in either agreement or disagreement, or by its ignoring them, one can identify with some certainty whom the author had in mind, or to what Reformed tradition he belonged, even though the *DDC* names neither the opponent nor his work.

Such extensive quotation of biblical proof texts within his argument to prove each detail is the most characteristic idiosyncrasy of the author of *DDC*. In his "Epistle" to his readers he emphasizes this fact: "I ... have striven to cram my pages even to overflowing, with quotations drawn from all parts of the Bible" (6.122). Doing so has, however, produced an unreadable book. An example of such textual overkill is the two-page consideration of contentment (6.728–30), which quotes 26 biblical passages to illuminate its simple subject. Only the adoption of italic print for the inserted quotations and contrasting roman for the author's own statements makes it possible, by ignoring the quotations unless one wants to verify a text, to get through the work. By varying his handwriting each scribe of the original manuscript gave the same signal to his audience. Today only Christopher Hill seems ready to champion its readability against that of other seventeenth century theological treatises,[5] which do not put off their audiences by such excessive numbers of quotations (*DDC* contains over 8,000 of them). Other authors either added their references in the margins or included them, sometimes without the texts or with a short paraphrase, within the body of the work.

It may be instructive to consider a single example, the rather simple treatment in book 1, chapter 22, "Of Justification," developed from St. Paul's description of man's salvation: those whom God "did foreknow, he also did predestinate. . . . Moreover, whom he did predestinate, them he also called; and whom he called, them he also justified; and whom he justified, them he also glorified" (Romans 8.29–30). The general organization of this chapter of the treatise (6.485–94) depends (as is typical) upon that of Wolleb's *Compendium*, here its book 1, chapter 30.[6] *DDC* includes in this chapter over 80 biblical quotations, some repeated and some consisting of more than one verse. Most are from the New Testament.

Only about a fourth of them derive from Wolleb's discussion of the subject. His *Compendium* cites about 33 passages, several more than once. Each of its references stands within its text, not in marginal notes; and most quote only the phrase from each that is significant for the argument—a readable and immediately verifiable text. Of *DDC*'s 80-odd citations,

21 parallel Wolleb's; the large remainder chronicle in their textual excesses the considerable individual labors of their author. For comparison one may consider the treatment of the same subject in the *Westminster Confession of Faith*, 11.[7] There 57 texts are cited, all being in the margins and none including any words from their biblical sources. Presbyterians evidently were expected to do their own homework.

DDC thus stands apart because of its huge number of proof texts, all included in the body of the book and almost all given in full. Obviously its author disapproved of the *Westminster* style. So did Milton. In *Hirelings* he decries the arguments of his antagonist, William Prynne, as one "whom ye may know by his wits lying ever beside him in the margent, to be ever beside his wits in the text" (7.294). Nor did Milton employ marginal notes like Prynne or *Westminster*. One may argue from such stylistic similarities a single authorship of treatise and canon. But the model that Wolleb furnished is quite compatible with Milton's practices in this respect and adequate to account for that of Wolleb's follower, the author of *DDC*, though the latter alone took it to the extremes that we must skim today. If the author of the treatise had been Milton's student, he may have picked up this stylistic preference from his teacher.

In several passages in the canonical prose Milton discusses, with proof texts, subjects that appear in the treatise and that also subjoin them. Comparison of the parallel citations is instructive. Obviously, had he composed both at about the same time the texts quoted on a common subject should be pretty much the same. When he was supposedly working on *DDC* in 1658 to 1660 he was certainly and simultaneously concerned with publication of *Of Civil Power* and *Hirelings* in 1659. But their citations are only partially congruent with those of the treatise. To take the most startling example, a major proof text that Milton analyzed at length in *Hirelings* is Genesis 14.18–20 and the New Testament interpretation of it in Hebrews 7.1–10. They concern the priest Melchizedek, to whom Abram paid a tenth of all his booty (a "tithe") after a military raid. Milton's opponents in this canonical work were the Anglican Henry Spelman and the Presbyterian William Prynne, both of whom had argued from Abram's tithing to Melchizedek the authority for requiring that everyone tithe to the Church.[8] The reason for its importance is that Abram's actions were pre-Mosaic and thus were argued to be binding on everyone, whereas the Mosaic laws that require tithing were judged to apply only to Jews. In *Hirelings* the issue is so important that Milton devotes three full pages to it (7.285–87). But the section on tithing in *DDC*, which also opposed the requirement (6.597–600), makes no mention at all of the example of Melchizedek,[9] who is only once alluded to elsewhere in the treatise and then merely as a model of priesthood (6.517). Granted that the treatise was not answering Spelman or Prynne; still Milton had been occupied with their position probably since 1653, when it seems that the first draft of *Hirelings* was set down.[10] It is inconceivable that a few years later he would completely ignore the issues raised by the account in Genesis, to which his tract responds at such length. But because the treatise is addressed to a Continental audience where the tithing model of Melchizedek did not carry such significance, its author ignores an example that had been so important in the English debate.

There are other divergences between *Hirelings* and *DDC* where differing sets of proof texts are used to support identical points. One commonplace attack on the practice of tithing was that it was based on ministers' love of money. In his tract Milton relies on eight proof texts: Acts 20.29, Titus 1.11, 2 Peter 2.3, 1 Timothy 6.5, 2 Timothy 4.3, Acts 20.30, 2 Peter 2.15, and Jude 11 (7.280). The equivalent passage in *DDC* cites only the first two of these in a collection of about a dozen (6.598–600). Or, to take another example, Milton rather reluctantly admits in *Hirelings* that some "recompense ought to be given" ministers, citing a single proof text, Luke 10.7 (7.281). *DDC* is more openhanded: "some remuneration is allowable" with proof citations from Matthew 10.10, 1 Corinthians 9.7–13, Galatians 6.6, 1 Timothy 5.7, 18, and 1 Corinthians 9.14; but there is no mention of the verse from Luke (6:595). The idea that ministers should be supported by voluntary contributions of their congregations finds expression in both canon (7.309–10) and treatise (6.597), but each is supported differently. In favor of this principle both quote Luke 10.7 and 8, and Phillipians 4.15 or 16–18. Then they diverge. *Hirelings* relies on Matthew 10.7–8 and Hebrews 13.16, *DDC* on Matthew 10.11 and 22.35, and 2 Corinthians 11.9. Treatise and canon cannot be harmonized in this regard though they were supposedly produced at the same time.

A similar lack of congruence appears in *Of Civil Power*. Both it and *DDC* agree on the power of the church to excommunicate members but with the hope that they will repent. They also agree on four texts that support such power: Matthew 18.17, 1 Corinthians 5.5 and 16.22, and 1 Timothy 1.20. But *Of Civil Power* cites an additional four texts peculiar to it, and *DDC*, eight that are different. A single author would not support a position simultaneously in such different ways.

In his treatment of blasphemy in *Of Civil Power*, Milton quotes only a single verse, Mark 9.39 and then relies on Parliament's definition in *The Act against several Atheistical, Blasphemous, and Execrable Opinions* of 9 August 1650 (7.246). *DDC* does not mention the verse from Mark (it appears once in a completely different context, 6.571) but, lacking the authority of the *Act*, cites over two dozen other texts to define the idea (6.698–700).

Heresy was linked to blasphemy in the seventeenth century mind. Milton's considerations of heresy appear in various publications, the earliest being *Areopagitica*. There he defines it as any blind or unthought-out belief even though it may happen to be true (2.543). The communicant's failure to reflect, not the belief itself, is the distinguishing factor: "A man may be a heretic in the Truth," and the Papist is listed as typical among such heretics. There are no proof texts. In the long analysis of the subject in *Of Civil Power* (7.247–53), Milton disposes of the original meaning of the Greek as "no word of evil note [the Authorized Version translates the texts containing it merely as sect], without censure or blame"; his proof texts are Acts 15.5 and 26.5. Or the word may mean "schism," 1 Corinthians 11.18, 19. It is the "choise" only of one opinion before another. The heretic, he goes on, is one "who maintains traditions or opinions not probable by scripture"—not thought through, that is, and most obviously again the Papist. Such heretics may be excommunicated, the proof text being Titus 3.10. Some (e.g., the Presbyterians in chapter 23 of their *Westminster Confession*) have delegated this power to the civil magistrate, using Romans 13 for their authority—to Milton's great distress.

His final statement about heresy appears in *Of True Religion* (8.421–23): it is "Religion taken up and believ'd from the traditions of men and additions to the word of God." Again, "Papacy is the only or the greatest Heresie." He concludes that "Heresie is in the Will and choice [and one must remember Milton's dictum, 'Reason also is choice'] profestly against Scripture,"—in comparison with mere error, which derives from misunderstanding the Scripture "after all sincere endeavours to understand it rightly." To avoid heresy one must diligently study the Bible, seeking "by prayer for Illumination of the holy Spirit." Although heresy is defined in different ways in these three statements spanning almost three decades, Milton's understanding of it remains essentially the same: it is the uncritical or unexamined acceptance of any dogma. One's beliefs must derive from reasoned consideration of biblical texts, not from any external authority. This is a basic Protestant position, expressed in the popular dictum, "Every man a priest." The all-pervasive example of the heretic in every one of Milton's statements on the subject is the Roman Catholic. Except for Acts 15.5 and 26.5, 1 Corinthians 11.18, 19, and Titus 3.10, there are no proof texts.

In considerations of this subject, *DDC* concludes its introductory Epistle with a very different definition of heretics as "only those people who *caused divisions of opinions and offenses contrary to the teaching of the Apostles*" (citing Romans 16.17–18) and then limits the definition to anything that contradicts the New Testament (6.123). Accordingly, its author naively claims to have followed only the lead of the Bible—not recognizing (as Milton did) that the real issue lay in how one thoughtfully came to understand the holy text, not in its thoughtless acceptance. *DDC* justifies its stance by a quotation from Paul, Acts 24.14, a verse Milton never mentions in his discussions of the subject. It is notable that the treatise makes no mention of the Roman Catholic issue that Milton raises forcefully every time he touches the subject.

When the author of the treatise next considers heretics, in book 1, chapter 31 (6.603–4), he finds their origin in "their own evil disposition . . ., or because some unnecessary restriction has been placed upon the church," with the textual citation of Phillipians 1.16 and Matthew 9.16. There is nothing in common (including proof texts) between this superficial definition and Milton's strong affirmation of every individual's responsibility for the reflective understanding of his own faith.

Neither edition of *Readie and Easie Way* (1660) offers any evidence of differing proof texts, because its subject matter and method of argument are so different from those of *DDC*. But some years later in 1673 Milton published his last important public effort, *Of True Religion*, which does match with some of the contents of *DDC* and which does rely on proof texts. Here the evidence leads to much the same conclusions as those drawn above from the proof texts of the 1659 tracts. However, this evidence may suggest a more direct correspondence between those proof texts of the tract and those of the treatise. For example, on the subject of rejecting other religious traditions, Milton cites in *Of True Religion* three proof texts: Galatians 1.8, Deuteronomy 4.2, and Revelation 22.18–19 (8.479). All three appear among nine cited on the same subject in *DDC* (6.591). It is important to note that an unidentified amanuensis added to the original text of the treatise the reference to Deuteronomy 4:2 (6.829), perhaps at Milton's own direction, if in 1673 he were consulting the proofs offered for this subject in the treatise and knew of another he thought should be included. Again, on the topic of idol worship as unenlightening for Christians, *Of True Religion* relies on four texts (8.433); two of these (Jeremiah 10.8 and Habakkuk 2.18) are included among the four cited in *DDC* on this subject (6.693). Further, in arguing that one should know scripture well enough to evaluate its teachers, *Of True Religion* employs three proof texts, Ephesians (wrongly identified as "Eccles.") 4.14, Acts 17.11 and Revelation 2.2 (8.435), which all appear among about a dozen on this topic in the treatise (6.601).

Lastly, *Of True Religion* concludes with a few biblical texts that spell out the doom awaiting transgressors, citing "*Romans 2d*" (which Keith Stavely, its editor, refers to Romans 1.21–32), 2 Thessalonians 2.11–12 (corrected by the editor from 1 Thessalonians) and Isaiah 44.18 (8.440). The first two are included among the larger series on this subject that ends book 1, chapter 4 of *DDC* (6.201–2).

Thus there may be more interdependence of treatise and this late tract than appears in Milton's earlier pamphlets. From the several convergences cited here, I conclude that in 1673 Milton may have used the Picard text of the treatise as a convenient concordance for quotations, and perhaps for ideas. Because it turned up among his effects, we know that the work was in his possession when he died the next year. But the diverging evidence of the proof texts cited in those tracts published in 1659 suggests that he did not find it a useful reference work then.

Finally, mention must be made of the fact that some of the biblical citations in *Of Civil Power, Hirelings*, and *Of True Religion* are wrong. One major error ("*Romans 2d*") probably owes to the compositor (8.440). The others represent a faulty memory of the exact text. Sometimes a chapter or verse is wrong, and one is a misunderstanding of Milton's dictation by his amanuensis (7.246). As notes to the Yale edition make clear, there are six such errors in the first tract, three in the second, and six in the third. The

Visitation Unimplor'd

general accuracy of these texts is a remarkable achievement for a blind man, but it does have these errors. Proportionately, though I have not made a census, there are far fewer in the treatise. It is not clear how Milton could have managed, blind, the much greater accuracy of the multitudinous proof texts it cites.

Chapter Seven

Divine Filiation

Because the heterodox view of the Son of God argued at length in *DDC* has been assigned to Milton's works, especially *Paradise Lost*, ever since the manuscript was recovered in the Public Record Office, I am going to consider here in some detail the conflicting issues that the treatise raises. The problem posed is not insignificant. Barbara Lewalski, for example, has, with several details based on this issue, objected to my thesis distancing Milton from the treatise.[1] She easily proves that in it "the Father alone is the supreme, self-existent, eternal God" but the Son "is not self-existent, not co-eternal, not of the same essence with the Father, not eternally generated of God's nature but 'voluntarily created or generated or produced . . . before all things.'" The Son's "divine nature and powers are not his own but derived from the Father." He is "mutable and not always omniscient." Her conclusion, with which I fully agree, is that "this is close to Arius and Socinus", except that in *DDC* "the Son shares in the Father's substance" as indeed is true. Furthermore, although she does not mention this,[2] so in the treatise does all creation. Thus the Son is in this respect like every other created being because everything derives *ex deo*. She goes on to point out similar ideas in *Paradise Lost* so as to prove a common author. There, she observes, the Son is not omniscient, he is mutable, he receives divine power from the Father, and God is "alone/From all Eternity," equalled by no other being. Finally, in *Paradise Regained*, Jesus does not know the purpose of his being led into the wilderness, another denial of omniscience. Such observations require, I think, reconsideration of some details.

First, it is important to see what Milton himself says about the Arianism and Socinianism with which he has been charged. Early references in his prose works (1.155, 533, 557, 685; 2.604; 3.507) are, as one would expect from the theologically conservative early Milton, uniformly unacceptive of their doctrines. But in *Of True Religion* (1673), dating from a few years after the time when he supposedly was actively at work on the treatise, one long sentence stands out. It is in a text that seeks to marshall Protestants of whatever stripe against what Milton sees as the immediate dangers of "the growth of Popery." Not surprisingly, although the tract is clearly conceived within the Anglican ("our") Church, it seeks toleration of non-Catholic groups, even Arians and Socinians, against what he views as the imminent dangers of Rome. Because of his narrow definition of heresy, such non-Anglicans are "no Hereticks" (8.423), and he goes on to point out how Anglicans can tolerate such deviances:

> The Lutheran holds Consubstantiation; an error indeed, but not mortal. The Calvinist is taxt with Predestination, and to make God the Author of sin; not with any dishonourable thought of God, but it may be over zealously asserting his absolute power, not without plea of Scripture. The Anabaptist is accus'd of Denying Infants their right to Baptism; again they say, they deny nothing but what the Scripture denies them. The Arian and Socinian are charg'd to dispute against the Trinity: they affirm to believe the Father, Son, and Holy Ghost, according to Scripture and the Apostolic Creed; as for terms of Trinity, Triniunity, Coessentiality, Tripersonality, and the like, they reject them as Scholastic Notions, not to be found in Scripture, which by a general Protestant Maxim is plain and perspicuous abundantly to explain its own meaning in the properest words, belonging to so high a Matter and so necessary to be known; a mystery indeed in their Sophistic Subtilties, but in Scripture a plain Doctrine. (8.424–25)

The long and complicated final sentence is difficult to understand, but can be read as tolerative of "the Arian and Socinian" as did the editor of the tract, Keith Stavely, in the Yale edition (8.425, nn. 24–26).

Bishop Burgess, who argued vigorously that Milton had nothing to do with *DDC*, had trouble interpreting this final sentence. To counter its apparent if perhaps obscure toleration of such doctrines, he proposed that its punctuation was inexact but could be cleared up by repointing it with parentheses: "The Arian and Socinian are charg'd to dispute against the Trinity (they affirm . . . to be known); a mystery indeed in their Sophistic Subtilties, but in Scripture a plain Doctrine,"³ a reading that Stavely protested as forced, an effort to "support his theory of Milton's antipathy to antitrinitarianism" (8.414, n. 19).

Indeed, the long and internally complex parenthesis is still difficult to follow as it stands in Burgess's revision. But he was on the right path. The paragraph is a good example of a rhetorical strategy that Milton sometimes employed in his later years, the sentence by sentence statement of another's position followed immediately by his own response to it. In *Hirelings*, for example, he takes a stand against someone who believes that ministers should be paid for their services:

> At burials thir [the ministers'] attendance they alleage on the corps; all the guests do as much unhir'd: But thir praiers at the grave; superstitiously requir'd: yet if requir'd, thir last performance to the deceasd of thir own flock. But the funeral sermon: at thir choise: or if not, an occasion offerd them to preach out of season, which is one part of thir office. But somthing must be spoken in praise: if due, thir duty; if undue, thir corruption. (7.298–99)

A modern format makes Milton's meaning clear:

> [The view of those advocating pay for the services of ministers:] At burials thir attendance they alleage on the corps.

[Milton's response:] All the guests do as much unhir'd.

But thir praiers at the grave.

[Response:] Superstitiously requir'd, yet if requir'd, thir last performance to the deceasd of thir own flock.

But the funeral sermon.

[Response:] At thir choise . . ., etc.

Compositors had no standard format for such a dialogue. In *Of Civil Power* the same kind of argument is primarily indicated by contrast of italic type with roman for statement and response.[4] In the foregoing quotation from *Hirelings* it is primarily indicated by punctuation. A similar kind of division holds for the passage from *Of True Religion*:

[The view of a speaker pointing out alienating differences among Protestant groups:] The Lutheran holds Consubstantiation.

[Milton's response:] An error indeed but not mortal.[5]

The Calvinist is taxt with Predestination and to make God the Author of sin.[6]

[Response: They do it] not with any dishonourable thought of God. . . .

The Anabaptist is accus'd of Denying Infants their right to Baptism.[7]

[Response:] Again they say, they deny nothing but what the Scripture denies them.

The Arian and Socinian are charg'd to dispute against the Trinity.

[Response] They affirm to believe the Father, Son,

and Holy Ghost, according to Scripture and the Apostolic Creed.

As for terms of Trinity, Triniunity, Coessentiality, Tripersonality, and the like, they reject them as Scholastic Notions, not to be found in Scripture (which by a general Protestant Maxim is plain and perspicuous abundantly to explain its own meaning in the properest words, belonging to so high a Matter and so necessary to be known).

[Response:] A mystery indeed in their Sophistic Subtilties, but in Scripture a plain Doctrin.

Such a division of the sentences shows clearly that Milton recognizes the position of the Arians and Socinians but flatly rejects "their Sophistic Subtilties" to accept instead the "plain Doctrin" of Trinitarian scripture. Writing from the perspective of the Church of England, he no more identifies with them than with Lutherans or Baptists or Presbyterians. He thinks, however, that the Church should tolerate them, as it should all Protestant groups, as it struggles against the Roman Catholics. In summary, the canonic *Of True Religion*, dictated after the supposed dictation of *DDC*, rejects the treatise's arguments about the Son of God.

I move next to apply to the analysis the same comparison of proof texts that earlier has been shown to be informative, though Milton presents us with none on this subject because he never argued the status of the Son in any work. In comparison, it was a topic that engaged the author of *DDC* so strongly that he devoted the longest chapter of his book to it. There, as throughout the work, he based his conclusions on biblical texts. In book 1, chapter 5, the author of *DDC* confronted dogmatic arguments concerning the generally accepted views of the Son of God—with which he vehemently disagreed—by responding in detail to 14 proof texts upon which his unnamed opponents had relied. He recognizes three "principal texts" and eleven others that are less important (6.238–49). By comparing his texts with those cited by his opponents, we can come to some identification of who they were, and we can recognize the tradition that governed their choice of texts. For ease of recognition I have italicized texts that agree with those cited in *DDC* (See Table 1.).[8]

It is immediately evident that Polanus and the *Westminster Confession* were not the opponents, whereas the two editions of Ames and the works of Wolleb and Louis Cappel, especially the last, certainly fall within the author's line of vision. Furthermore, only the 1623 edition of Ames includes Jude 4, which suggests that first edition drew his attention rather than the later one. Cappel alone mentions Hebrews 1.8, one of the "major" texts for rebuttal. Considering how frequently *DDC* refers to Ames and Wolleb elsewhere, their appearance here is no surprise. Cappel as a third major source is more unexpected, since he is cited only once elsewhere in the treatise for his commentary upon 1 Corinthians 11.4 (6.673). But, as noted earlier, he was a leader of the school at Saumur, with which the author of *DDC* seems to have had important ties, a relationship reinforced by his response here to Cappel's arguments.

As I have mentioned, this chapter on the subject of

Table 1

DDC	Polanus	Ames 1623	Ames 1627	Wolleb	Westminster	Cappel
John 1:1	John 1:14	Rev 1:11	John 1:1	John 1:1	1 John 5:7	John 1:1
John 20:28	1:18	1 John 5:20	Rom 9:5	17:3	Matt 3:16	20:28
Heb 1:8	1:34	Titus 2:13	1 Tim 3:16	20:31	28:19	1 Tim 3:16
	3:16	Jude 4	Rev 17:14	Acts 20:28	2 Cor 13:14	Acts 20:28
Matt 1:23	Matt 3:17	Rom 9:5		Rom 9:5	John 12:14	Heb 1:8
Acts 16:31	2 Cor 1:19	Rev 19:6		Titus 2:13	1:18	Titus 2:13
16:34	Luke 1:31	Rev 17:1				Rom 9:5
20:28	Rom 1:4				John 1:1	1 John 5:20
Rom 9:5					1:14	
1 Tim 3:16					1 John 5:20	
Titus 2:13					Phil 2:6	
1 John 3:16					Gal 4:4	
5:20						
Phil 2:6						
Jude 4						

the Son is by far the longest, most vigorously argued, and most obviously heterodox one in the treatise. That *DDC*'s author recognized this chapter's obvious prominence in his work is evident in the fact that it alone has a defensive preface. But Milton himself is completely silent on this subject in all his canonical writings; accordingly, there are no collections of proof texts to compare with those just enumerated from *DDC*. Because he never mentions it, this major Christian issue was not debateable for him, as it was for the author of the treatise. Indeed, early in his career in the "Nativity Ode" he praises the Son, who sits amidst Trinitarian unity (line 11) in completely orthodox fashion. In his later maturity he invokes the Trinity to inspire *Paradise Lost*,[9] identifying each of its members by a physical location recognized by all Christians. First the Father, who

> on the secret top
> Of *Oreb*, or of *Sinai*, didst inspire
> That Shepherd [Moses], who first taught the chosen
>   seed,
> In the Beginning how the Heav'ns and Earth
> Rose out of *Chaos* (I, 6–10).

"Or" (the coordinate conjunction is significant) the Son, closely identified with "*Sion* Hill" in Jerusalem,
> and *Siloa's* Brook that flow'd
> Fast by the Oracle of God (11–12),

where Jesus restored sight to a blind man (John 9.7). "And chiefly" (again the coordinate conjunction) the Holy Spirit

> that dost prefer
> Before all Temples th' upright heart and pure.
> (17–18)

To the contrary *DDC* clearly asserts that the Spirit is not to be thus invoked (6.295).

In *Paradise Lost*, the Son alone is hailed in the invocation to book 3 as "Holy Light" (in John 8.14 he is "the Light of the World") and described as coeternal with the Father or as his firstborn.[10] The three-day War in Heaven at the center of the poem, covered in books 5 and 6, recounts in allegorical fashion the victory of the Son over death in the three-day period from Good Friday to Easter.[11] Finally, in the last invocation, that to book 7, the Holy Spirit is again invoked, now as the feminine Urania. "Spirit" in Hebrew is "ruach," a feminine noun. (Properly speaking, the poem to book 9 is not an invocation: divine inspiration now has become a constant presence with the poet, attending him as a "visitation unimplor'd," l. 22.) The three invocations, I conclude, Milton meant as prayers to the Trinity.

Elsewhere in Milton's writings the Son also receives divine honors. In *Of Civil Power* he asserts with perfect orthodoxy that the saved are "bought and by him redeemd who is God" (7.264), an unquestioning assertion of the divinity of the Son. The next year he concludes *Readie and Easie Way* by praying that neither "Thou . . . who didst create mankind free; nor Thou next, who didst redeem us from being servants of men" will "suffer" his pleas in this work to be ignored (7.463).

Again, in *Paradise Lost* the Son foresees that he will yield to death, but only "All that of me can die" (3.246)—only the human nature, that is, in the orthodox tradition. The author of the treatise tends to the view that the divine nature dies too: "A lot of passages in the Bible make his divine nature succumb to death along with his human nature" with the conclusion that "The whole of a sacrifice [must] be killed. So it follows that Christ, the sacrificial lamb, was totally killed" (6.439–40).

Whether or not some aspects of *Paradise Lost* are fully Trinitarian is, however, certainly questionable. In book 3 the Son is ignorant of much of the future in his dialogue with the Father. In a long speech (3.144–66) he questions whether mankind should finally be lost because of its own folly, whether Satan will be finally successful, and whether God will destroy his own creation. These are not the utterances of omniscience. The Father responds that mankind must indeed perish unless some worthy sacrifice can be found, concluding, "Dwels in all Heaven charitie so dear?" (l. 216). But such a question puts his own omniscience into question too, or is it only a literary device to elicit the Son's response? If the latter is true, then the Son's apparently ignorant earlier query may be uttered with a similar purpose. The Son's limited knowledge in this part of the dialogue, that is, may mean no more than does the Father's; it is rather a perhaps awkward attempt on the Milton's part to outline the salvific aspects of the rest of his poem, with unfortunate consequences for divine prescience. The Son is not necessarily subordinate here, though one may so understand this passage.

But toward the end of the colloquy the Father is revealed as alone omnipotent. After the resurrection of the God/man, the Son will "reign forever" as recipient from the Father of all divine power (3.315–17). From the lines that follow, this transfer of power seems to be made with the Last Judgment in mind. Again, earlier in the chronology of the poem but later in the text, the Father decrees that "This day I have begot [i.e., exalted; see below] My onely Son," raising him thereby to command over all the angels (5.603–6), another endowment of a subordinate being by a superior one. A third time, at dawn on the third day of the War in Heaven, the Father declares that "such Vertue and Grace/Immense [unmeasurable] I have transfer'd" into the Son that he will be invincible against Satan and his evil army (6.703–05). Then at the creation of the Universe in book 7 (165–66), the Father "send[s] along" his "overshadowing Spirit and might" with the Son to effectuate it. Such transfers of divine power clearly demonstrate that the Son is subordinate in power to the Father, not a characteristic of the traditional triune Godhead. But such subordinationism, as Patrides, Adamson and I have argued,[12] has a worthy history in early Christianity and stands at a great distance from the Arianism or Socinianism of the treatise. To respond to Lewalski's final point, Jesus' ignorance as to why he was being led into the wilderness in *Paradise Regained* merely reflects the ignorance of his human element, the divine having been laid aside or "emptied" in this respect at the Incarnation.[13]

As was proved by two and a half centuries of readers before the recovery of the manuscript of *DDC*, almost everyone found orthodoxy in the poem. It may, of course, be read otherwise; Richardson, Defoe, and others made the charge of heresy early in the eighteenth century.[14] But these problems grew out of their misunderstanding of certain words: that the Father "begot" the Son they understood as "originated" in the usual modern meaning of the word ("This day I have begot whom I declare/My onely son," 5.603–4). Or they understood that he was created (the Son is "of all creation first," 3.383); or the Father exists in solitary primacy "alone" ("th' Almighty" tells Adam that "I . . . am alone/From all eternitie, for none I know/Second to me or like, equal much less" (8.405–07). But Milton is thinking in all such examples of specific biblical texts that, because they are biblical, cannot be heretical but require special meanings to avoid such interpretations. "Beget" in one special significance derives from Psalm 2, as it is interpreted by Paul (Acts 13.33), and by the author of Hebrews (1.5; 5.5), as the Son's exaltation or anointing to messiahship. Thus *Paradise Lost* book 5, lines 603–04. In another sense, it means something like "be part of" as in the Nicene statement that Christ is "the only-begotten Son of God, begotten of the Father before all worlds . . ., begotten, not made," a dogma never challenged by Milton in the canonic works. In *DDC*, on the other hand, its author defines "beget" via Revelation 3.14 in the modern sense, as the Father's having "created or generated or produced the Son before all things" (6.211). This text states that John saw a figure taken to be Christ who said he is "the beginning of the creation of God," where "beginning" must for the orthodox be understood in the sense of "activation." "Firstborn" may mean "originator of" in Colossians 1.15–17: the Son is "The firstborn of every creature, for by him were all things created . . . and he is before all things." *DDC* argues against and rejects the orthodox interpretations of both Revelation 3.14 and Colossians 1.15 in its account of creation (6.302, 303), but the latter text underlies the alternative invocation of the Son, the light of God, as "Ofspring of Heav'n first-born" or "coeternal beam" of the eternal God, the uncreated "Bright effluence" of an uncreated "bright essence" (3.1–5). It is striking that these metaphors, well attested as descriptive of the Trinity for early church fathers, do not appear anywhere in the treatise, prominent though they are in the poem. But then it sedulously avoids everywhere all figures of speech.

Concerning this last point, H.R. MacCallum built an interesting case for Milton's supposed opposition to the use of figurative interpretations of scripture, his primary authority being the practices found in *DDC*.[15] Thus he understood a sentence in *Of Reformation* ("men came to scan the *Scripture* by the Letter," 1.522) as a plea for faith rather than for the figurative reading of such language—though I question whether this is Milton's meaning here, MacCallum having been led astray by the rigidly unfigurative treatise. Aside from Milton's employment of powerful metaphors like "Bright Essence," there is his ready acceptance of texts as embodying "types" or "shadows" or "figures" that include metaphorical meanings.[16] His thesis forced MacCallum to question such insightful books as F.M. Krouse's *Milton's Samson and the Christian Tradition* and Rosamund Tuve's *Images and Themes in Five Poems by Milton*, many of whose arguments are based upon metaphorical understandings of Milton's texts.

As for Lewalski's point that the Son is mutable, as in his being "begotten" (i.e., exalted above the angels) in 5.600ff., the orthodox understanding of his immutability applies only to the moral aspects of his being: he is sinless (though tempted in *Paradise Regained*). Of course he changes otherwise, most obviously in his union with man in the Incarnation. Her next point to be answered is that, speaking to Adam, the voice who is "alone/From all Eternitie" (8.405) is that of the solitary Father. But Milton reflects a widely accepted interpretation of Genesis 2.18 ("The Lord God said, 'It is not good that man should be alone'") which has been taken to imply that to the contrary it is good that God be alone. For Jews, this supported monotheism, for Christians, the Trinity, because the Godhead ("Lord God") was taken as speaking here as indeed it had acted as a unit in the creation narrated in chapter 1 of Genesis. The "God" who acted there is the Hebrew plural "Elohim." Probably the same is to be understood of the creation described in book 7 of *Paradise Lost* where the Son is the apparent agent but where the creative Word is also called "The Almighty"—the Godhead, in other words (339).

Such or similar interpretations of these and other problematic biblical passages may strike modern readers as badly forcing the meaning of the text, but they were adopted to preserve orthodoxy, and so readers of *Paradise Lost* accepted them until the discovery of *DDC*, which I believe in every case understands them in what we today probably find a more natural though heterodox meaning. Because everyone thought that Milton had written the treatise and thus authorized readers to transfer to his canonic writings each more natural reading from it, such interpretations have understandably convinced many of his heterodoxy in the genuine works. Few today are interested in the kind of theological distinctions that used to occupy the reflections of the religious. On the other hand, if one rejects this return to the older orthodox definitions and accepts instead the patent heterodoxy of *DDC* as Milton's, one can make him out to be an extraordinarily subtle or devious author who had such double meanings in mind, though his "fit audience," who could understand his hidden messages, would indeed be very few until the recovered manuscript set them straight. Such an interpretation Lewalski well represents, concluding that in "*De Doctrina* . . . Milton argues his most heretical positions by amassing scripture texts" that he understood very differently from everyone else, including "his later orthodox Christian readers. That is why *De Doctrina* has proved so useful to so many Milton scholars."[17] To me it is incredible that he could disguise such heterodoxy so well that generations of readers were duped until the treatise was recovered.

Once Milton seems to have attacked one of the views argued in the unpublished manuscript that he had in his possession. The treatise defined the theological word "essence" as applied to the Trinity in terms of number—an interpretation that we can perhaps more readily recognize as "individuality." Its position is that "since a numerical difference is the result of a difference in essence, if two things are two numerically, they must also be two essentially" or two individuals (6.216), a major basis for its Arian argument distancing the Son from the Father because, as individuals, their essences must be different. In his *Art of Logic* Milton picks up the same idea (from Scaliger, he says), that "things which differ in number also differ in essence, and never do things differ in number without also differing in essence" (8.233)—seemingly a direct affirmation of the words quoted from the treatise. He then adds a sentence of his own that the editor of the work, Walter Ong, points out was not from his source in Ramus (8.233, n. 7). Milton emphasizes its importance by italics: *Here let the theologians take notice*, which has been understood to emphasize the same point that he, as assumed author, was making about essence in the unpublished treatise.[18] But Bishop Burgess protested right after the recovery of the manuscript that such is a misreading: Milton's warning instead is addressed to those who confuse the *two* meanings, not one, that the word "essence" may carry.[19] As the passage in the *Logic* continues, "the essence of anything is partly common [that is, what constitutes in this case the members of the Godhead] and partly proper [that is, what individuates them]; matter [or better, substance] constitutes the common essence [of the Trinity] and form the proper [essence of each of its three members]" (8.234). One must then beware of limiting the meaning of "essential" to its single "proper" sense, Milton continues: "From form alone comes the essential [that is, individuating] difference," for in the other meaning of the word they share a common essence or underlying substance. Ignoring these differences so as to limit essence to mean only the individuating or "proper" element led the author of *DDC* into denial of true Godhead for the Son.

In one important observation concerning the Son, *DDC* adopts a heretical position that cannot be matched in any way by reinterpretations of any of the texts of Milton's canonical works. This is its dogma that mankind can be saved by belief in the Father alone; anyone who is totally ignorant of the Son, like the good pagans, has as good title as devout Christians to the salvation which he offered in his sacrifice made for all: "Christ's perfect sacrifice is in every way sufficient even for those who have never heard of his name, but who only believe in God" (6.455). Thus "there are a lot of Jews, and Gentiles too, who are saved although they believed or believe in God alone" (6.425). Such a position is understandable in a work whose Arianism denies to the Son a necessary intermediary role between man and God. To the contrary, in *Paradise Lost* "to God [there] is no access/Without Mediator" (12.239–40), whom the virtuous pagans, of course, could not know; and in *Paradise Regained*, beginning with Socrates, they were led only "by Natures light," were "Ignorant of themselves, of God much more" (4.228–310). Not being aware of the Christian God, they could not be saved. There is, however, no evidence that Milton would have excluded from grace the Old Testament patriarchs in this group.

Paired with the Trinity in Christian orthodoxy is the dogma of the Incarnation: the means and the meaning of the union of the Son of God with man in the historical Jesus. To respond to a variety of interpretations of this dogma that had grown up in the early church and were, like the issues over the Trinity, threatening to split it, the Council of Chalcedon (451) definitively affirmed that in the Incarnation "truly God and truly man" united—their two natures, Godhead and Manhood, being joined without "the distinction of natures being . . . taken away, but rather the property of each nature bring preserved, and concurring in one Person."[20] Whenever Milton refers to this dogma in *Paradise Lost*, it is with unexceptionable orthodoxy. Thus the Father instructs the Son, "Thir [mankind's] Nature also to thy Nature joyn," to become a "Man among men" (3.282–83). Later he foretells that the Son will join "Manhood to Godhead" (12.389). In dogmatic terms the emphasis upon human nature rather than a person has been viewed as central in that all humanity participates (as manhood) in the Resurrection, not just the single man Jesus.

The treatise, on the other hand, defines these words quite otherwise (book 1, chapter 19). Human nature for its author cannot be divorced from the human personality; thus when two natures, the divine and the human, joined, it was in his view a union of two already existing persons—the first example, I suppose, of what we would diagnose today as a case of dual personality. This was one of the main heresies, Nestorianism, that the Council at Chalcedon was trying to block. I have argued at length from the evidence of *DDC* that Milton was thus a Nestorian,[21] but all my evidence derived from the treatise, not from the canon, which does not provide a single supportive detail. Later, Lewalski, convinced by the treatise of Milton's Arianism, developed a second interpretation, again one that Milton's contemporaries would have considered heretical, a form of monophysitism. The two natures/persons that joined could result in the single nature/person of Jesus because the Arian Son of the treatise was not fully divine.[22] She too derived her evidence from the treatise, not from the canon.

As was true in his support of the Arian heresy in his treatise, its author defined his terms with modern meanings rather than with the specialized traditional ones upon which orthodoxy has been based. Schaff has made the point clearly with regard to the creed of Chalcedon:

> There is, no doubt, a serious difficulty in the old orthodox Christology, if we view it in the light of modern psychology. We can conceive of a human nature without sin (for sin is a corruption, not an essential quality, of man), but we can not conceive of a human nature without personality, or a self-conscious and

free Ego; for this distinguishes it from the mere animal nature.²³

For the Christian fathers, the words "nature" and "person" were not so nearly synonymous as they are for us. The author of *DDC* defined the elements making up the Trinity and the Incarnation in ways that appeal to us because they are also our meanings. He has overlooked, as we often have too, their original significance, which permitted one to understand biblical passages in an orthodox sense. As a result his work (attributed to John Milton) is now notorious for having redefined them in ways not acceptable to orthodoxy but more easily understood by modern readers somewhat unsophisticated in religious issues.

Chapter Eight

The Confounded Confusion of Chaos

A major subject to which the author of *DDC* bears witness is the denial of a dichotomized universe. Ever since Jack Adamson's essay, "Milton and the Creation," appeared in 1962[1] Milton's monism (argued from the treatise) has been a matter of near-creedal acceptance. In brief, Adamson used *DDC* to show that the substance of which God made the universe he did not create from nothing (*ex nihilo*) but from himself (*ex deo*). "It is clear," the author of the treatise asserts, "that the world was made out of some sort of matter [which] must either have always existed, independently of God, or else originated from God at some point in time" (6.307). He proceeds to show that the latter alternative is the necessary choice and goes on to the logical extension that, derived directly from God as it was, it was necessarily good: "this original matter was not an evil thing . . .: it was good, and it contained the seeds of all subsequent good. . . . It was in a confused and disordered state at first, but afterwards God made it ordered and beautiful" (6.308). Assuming, as everyone then did, that Milton was the author of these sentences, one would necessarily read their implications into the chaos of *Paradise Lost*, Raphael's description of the "Scale of Nature" which orders the universe, and the narration of its creation in book 7. Thus monism: matter underlies all being, including God, from whom it derives. But as Augustine pointed out, creation *ex deo* runs counter to the orthodox belief that only the Son was begotten (from eternity) from the divine substance: "You [God] created heaven and earth but you did not make them of your own substance. If you had done so, they would have been equal to your only-begotten Son, and therefore to yourself."[2] Such problems do not, of course, arise for an Arian like the author of *DDC*.

I propose to reconsider the evidence that *Paradise Lost* affords. (Milton never raises the issue of monism elsewhere. The *Art of Logic* discusses the material cause of things but does not argue the question of how matter originates.) It is clear that the material chaos in the poem must be equivalent to the original matter derived directly from God according to the treatise. But *DDC* says unequivocally that "it was good," a fact that cannot be asserted of its ruler Chaos in the poem, who is certainly not good. He is lawless ("Anarch old," 2.988), and his realm consists of total disorder, "confusion worse confounded" (2.996). Satan's trip through it is one of unremitting violence. Chaos welcomes the evil visitor and helps him go on to Earth, adding, "Havock and spoil and ruin are my gain" (2.1019), scarcely characteristics of goodness. He had opposed God's earlier creation of Hell, then of Heaven and Earth, out of his dominions and obviously would like for them to be reduced again to chaos. The only sense in which his realm, the physical chaos, can be described as good is as providing the materials from which God founds creation. As God he would not create an evil Deep but one with the potential of becoming evil, as was true of his creation of the angel who would become the evil Satan, and of Adam. I conclude with Michael Lieb that chaos is neutral: "The Abyss is not inherently evil, although it can be put to evil use."[3] I see no way to identify the chaos described in the poem with the inherent goodness of the original matter as the treatise defines it. As to whether it derives *ex nihilo* or *ex deo*, the poem is simply silent; and Milton never raises the question elsewhere.

Believing that the same author was responsible for both treatise and poem, some of our most perceptive critics have wrestled with the reconciliation of this conflict between them. For example, A.S.P. Woodhouse rather unwillingly conceded that in contrast with the description of it in *DDC* chaos could indeed be evil in the poem.[4] Significantly, Regina Schwartz has devoted an entire chapter to some aspects of the problem, seeking "some resolution to the conflict between Milton's doctrine [in *DDC*] and his depiction of it" in *Paradise Lost*, but she premised her discussion by giving up on its central problem: "I find the inference of an evil chaos so difficult to escape that it is not worth trying."[5] Of course, if Milton did not author the chapter on creation in the treatise, the problem vanishes.

In order to understand clearly the significance of the contrast between the inherently good chaos of *DDC* and the inherently neutral one of *Paradise Lost*, one must recognize that the latter exists in two distinct forms, all originally neutral, of which God transforms a part to good, the limited material upon which he will found his creation. This is the area that the Son encircles with the sweep of the golden compasses. At that action the "vast immeasurable Abyss/ Outrageous as a Sea, dark, wasteful, wilde" (7.211–12) changes with the concomitant command, "Silence, ye troubl'd waves, and thou Deep, peace" (7.216), marking the emergence of the second, now good, stage of the existence of chaos. In his account of this same event viewed from a different perspective, Uriel, the angel of the Sun, saw how "at his [God's] Word the formless mass . . . came to a heap"—separated off from the rest—and the "Confusion [of chaos] heard his voice" so that its "vast infinitude" would stand "rul'd [or] confin'd" (3.707–10). This limited area is the matrix of creation which becomes the orbicular and illuminated universe that Satan sees from the darkness of chaos as he ends his long journey through it (2.1034–39).

Even before this event and before the creation begins, the Father had directed and explained this transformation of a portion of the neutral chaos into one that provides the good matter for the universe: he directs his Son, the creative Word, to

> bid the Deep
> Within appointed bounds be Heav'n and Earth,
> Boundless the Deep, because I am who fill
> Infinitude, nor vacuous the space.
> Though I uncircumscrib'd my self retire,
> And put not forth my goodness, which is free
> To act or not, Necessitie and Chance
> Approach not mee, and what I will is Fate.
> (7.166–73)

Through the divine obscurity of this somewhat convoluted command, one perceives that the "Deep" is the original neutral chaos. It is "Boundless," as is God, but not identical with him. He claims responsibility for its origin and extent: infinite as he is, he has filled the Infinitude of a "Boundless ... Deep." This has been interpreted in accord with the dogma of the treatise: it "originated from God." But it may mean merely that he "fill[ed] Infinitude" with this creation without any implication that this entity originated from himself.

He goes on in the next sentence to explain that he did not have to extend to this original Deep or chaos his "goodness, which is free/To act or not," and thus it is not necessarily good as the author of *DDC* insists that it is. In these lines, that is, Milton is taking an express stand against the moral (and physical) monism inherent in the Deep which the treatise supports. God's retirement from it is moral, not physical; for he is not in the least material: "Necessitie and Chance," he says, do not "approach" him in any way, but they do determine matter. In chaos, which certainly is material, "*Chance* governs all" (2.910) and Chance is a companion of Chaos's throne (2.963). Thus God expressly denies himself any materiality, which is subject to chance. In sharp contrast, the all-encompassing material monism that the author of *DDC* postulates forbids such a distinction as Milton can make when he recognizes two stages in the existence of chaos.

Perhaps the most obvious difference between poem and treatise—one that is generally recognized and fundamental—is God's extended activity before the creation of the world in *Paradise Lost*, which begins following the passage at book 7, line 216: "Silence, ye toubl'd waves, and thou Deep, peace" and marks the first extension of divine goodness into the now-circumscribed area of chaos. Because heaven and its angels had existed before this event in the epic, the creation described in book 7 and in Genesis 1 does not for Milton mark the beginning of time. To the contrary, following Augustine, many biblical exegetes would agree "unreservedly [with him] that before he made heaven and earth, God made nothing"—the Bishop's serious answer to the question he had asked, "What was God doing before he made heaven and earth?" rather than the sarcastic response, "He was preparing Hell for people who pry into mysteries."[6] That Milton was aware of the fact that he was going against such general opinion is certain by his somewhat defensive statement in the Argument prefixed to book 1 explaining the existence of the fallen angels before any creation began: "that Angels were long before this visible Creation, was the opinion of many ancient Fathers." He certainly knew this Augustinian dogma as he violated it, for in *Tetrachordon* he had argued, "in the ecclesiastical stories one demanding how God imploy'd himself before the world was made, had answer; that he was making hel for curious questioners" (2.663), a direct paraphrase of the father. But Milton's citation then was only illustrative: he quotes this statement not for its dogmatic content but merely as an example of what we would call a "put-down argument" (Augustine himself terms it "frivolous"), which he goes on to say that he will not use. In sharp contrast, the author of *DDC* fully accepts this concept, denying any divine activity before the creation described in Genesis 1 begins and making it indeed the introduction to his chapter on the creation (6.299).

In his discussion of the creation of "things invisible" later in this chapter, however, *DDC's* author suggests—contradicting this earlier statement—that the divine dwelling place, heaven, was made "ages before" the beginning of the world (6.311), as were the angels. In close agreement with the Argument to book 1 of *Paradise Lost*, the author of the treatise writes, "Certainly many of the Greek Fathers, and some of the Latin, were of the opinion that angels ... existed long before this material world" and that their "apostasy ... took place before even [its] first beginnings" (6.313). One way to explain this sharp contradiction with the Augustinian view accepted earlier in the chapter is that, as was probably true in the later argument favoring divorce, Milton himself dictated an insertion that was entered into the manuscript. Skinner's copying of this part of the work effaced all evidence that it was so added.

Another account concerning the status of matter in the universe is Raphael's description (to Adam) of the Scale of Nature (5.469–90) or Chain of Being that unifies the circumscribed matter into which God extends his goodness. From it, the Divine has "downward purged/The black tartareous cold infernal dregs/Adverse to life" (7.237–39). The Angel elaborates the conception of a single matter that derives from God and is the substrate of everything (but he does not mention its earlier existence as undivided chaos—indeed, he does not mention chaos at all): "one Almightie is from whom/All things proceed" and back to whom they may ultimately return. They all result from the impregnation of the matter, common to everything, with the different forms that distinguish one being from another: the pre-existent matter has been "Indu'd with various forms" in "various degrees/Of substance (5.469–74)." At the beginning of the poem we learned that this impregnation happened when the "Spirit" induced these forms into matter: there the narrator invokes that Spirit who

> from the first
> Wast present, and with mighty wings outspred,
> Dove-like satst brooding on the vast Abyss
> And madst it pregnant . . . (1.19–22)

This activity is restated when the "brooding wings" infused the matter with "vital vertue . . . and vital warmth" as the creation begins in book 7 (235–36). But this matter, now constituting the "vast Abyss" or the matrix to be impregnated, is not the neutral original matter of chaos but that of its calmed and spatially restricted area to which God had extended his goodness with the sweep of the golden compasses.

The various levels of being which result from enduing matter with form, Raphael goes on to say, actively seek to rise to higher forms; thus the Scale of Nature results. "Body [may] up to spirit work." The root becomes the stalk, which in turn becomes the leaves and fruit. They, "by gradual scale sublim'd," may "To vital Spirits aspire, to animal,/To intellectual." This last level, the human, may then seek to rise to the yet higher, angelic, level (5.478–99). Thus the informed matter of food (body) may become a human being (spirit) or even an angel, who can find it nutritious as Raphael does. Literally, "Mann ist was Mann isst." In this way the angel, as Milton's spokesman, tries to bridge the mind-body dichotomy that exercised many contemporaries like Henry More, Ralph Cudworth, and René Descartes. The various levels of "spirits" that Raphael distinguishes determine the various levels of being; a single matter is common to everything.

I do not believe, however, that Raphael's declaration can withstand rigorous analysis. At its lower levels his "spirits" seem analogous to those postulated by contemporary science. According to Robert Burton, who is repeating the scientific commonplaces of the day, from digestion of food come the four humours, including blood. From blood, in turn, derives

"Spirit . . ., a most subtle vapour, which . . . is the instrument of the soul to perform all his actions; a common tie or *medium* betwixt the body and the soul, as some will have it."[7] According to him there are three levels of such spirits, "Natural, vital, animal," which Raphael seems to be echoing in part with his "vital, animal, and intellectual" spirits. But Burton always defines his in the physiological terms of life processes. Thus his *"animal spirits . . .* give sense and motion" to the body. Such spirits he evidently considered to be corporeal substances, though highly refined ones. It is just these physiological "animal spirits" derived from the blood, according to Burton, that Satan taints to produce Eve's dream in *Paradise Lost* (4.805).

Confusingly, Raphael skips Burton's "natural" spirit but retains his "vital" and "animal" ones and adds the yet higher "intellectual," which provides "understanding, whence the Soul/Reason receives, and reason is her being" (5.486–87). But understanding and reason are not physiological spirits; they are psychological faculties, as Adam explains to Eve:

> know that in the Soul
> Are many lesser Faculties that serve
> Reason as chief. (5.100–02)

Raphael thus must mean that reason is the identifying activity of the human soul, not identical with it as "her being." As Burton again observes, "The common division of the *soul* is into three principal faculties, *vegetal, sensitive,* and *rational.*"[8] For him too they are faculties, not spirits in the physiological sense; and they must be what Raphael is driving at with his "vital, animal, and intellectual" spirits.

Like Burton, but unlike Raphael, the treatise defines spirit in this context as faculty. *DDC* observes that in the Bible the word "means nothing but the breath of life"—the incorporeal substance upon which Burton will elaborate in his long "Digression" upon spirits as demons and witches—"or the vital or sensitive or rational faculty" (6.317)—identical with Burton's "three principal faculties." The treatise is clear; Raphael's words are not—because of Milton's eagerness through Raphael as mouthpiece to unify the entire creation from the lowest to the highest informed matter into a single chain of being. Raphael's reason is not a substance but is rather the identifying ability or faculty possessed by one substance, the human soul. Satan accurately repeats this traditional series of faculties: "Growth, Sense, Reason,/ All summ'd up in Man" (9.113). Raphael confuses the physiological and corporeal meanings of "spirits" with the "spirits" that are synonymous with souls and yet higher forms of incorporeal substance.[9]

DDC appears superficially to be arguing the same monistic position: it asserts that matter "originated from God at some point in time" (6.307), and thus "it was good, and contained all the seeds of all subsequent good" (6.308). From its full-blown materialistic monism Lewalski can argue that this same "principle underlies the epic's blurred distinction between matter and spirit, angels and humans, intuitive and discursive intellect"[10]—blurred distinctions that certainly exist in the poem. But as has been seen, it cannot account for its primitive neutral chaos. Furthermore, there is no evidence at all in *DDC*'s chapter on creation to support the concept of a Scale of Nature or Chain of Being; nor does it give any indication that body may actively work its way up to higher forms as Raphael says it "aspires" to do.

One may posit against this last statement the importance that the treatise places in this chapter upon the "power of matter." It asserts that "all forms—and the human soul is a kind of form—is produced from [not by] the power of matter [*ex potentia materiae*]" (6.325). This seems at first sight to be directly analogous to matter that can work its way, in Raphael's words, up to vital, animal, and intellectual spirits. Such, however, is a profound misunderstanding of the meaning of "power" as a translation of *potentia materiae*.[11] The concept derives from Aristotle, who viewed all being as composed of matter and form. Matter, in his view, had the capacity or potentiality (the true meaning here of *potentia*) to become a formed object. In itself matter is completely powerless, inert. Another being *educes* from it the object which it potentially can become. In no sense can it "aspire" to anything in Raphael's sense. The newly formed object educed from it (not induced into it) can in turn be the matter from which a yet higher form may be educed, and so on. A chain of being, that is, is possible in Aristotle's system, but its constituents do not, *qua* matter, seek such higher realization. Finally, the matter in Raphael's system is "Indu'd" with externally derived forms. Milton in his poem and the author of the treatise, in conclusion, arrive at a monistic universe from quite different fundamentals. Milton's is spatially limited by the "golden compasses," which "circumscribe/This Universe and all created things" (7.225–27) but exclude the rest of chaos from which it derives. The treatise never alludes in any way to a Scale of Nature; Milton in turn never mentions the power of matter. In such attempted monism neither satisfactorily resolved the mind-body dualism that troubled contemporaries. Through Raphael, Milton tries to achieve it at the expense of confusing two different meanings of spirit. The treatise asserts monism with the concomitant failure to distinguish the created from the divine.

One should note that Raphael establishes the concept of the Scale of Nature to prove what may seem to be a rather minor point: that he can really eat and digest human food. The issue had been settled for all angelologists except Milton: angels merely seemed to eat.[12] But he insists that Adam, Eve and Raphael sat down

> And to their viands fell, nor seemingly
> The Angel, nor in mist, the common gloss
> Of Theologians. (5.434–36)

This derives directly from Genesis 18.1–8, where Abraham entertains angels at a meal, the scriptural authority for Milton's views on this subject. Had he written *DDC* he could have found this passage a useful support for the argument presented there for creation *ex deo*, the proof being clearly implied in this biblical text. The author of the treatise was evidently not interested in angels' food or in the fact that it could support his position.

There is indeed no such biblical authority for angelic sexuality. A basic reason for religious authorities to reject it is their belief that the primary reason for sexuality is the begetting of children; such, for example, has been the position of the Roman Catholic Church. Angelic sex would lead to the production of baby angels who would, I suppose, upset heaven's economy; and putti are useful only as decorative appendages to renaissance pictures. The author of *DDC* seems to have accepted some such dogma emphasizing the fertile aspect of sexuality in human beings. For him the "proper fruit of marriage" is "the procreation of children." Since the fall of Adam, the relief of sexual desire has become "a kind of secondary end" (6.370).[13] In contrast, in the poem, before the fall of Adam it obviously had been a primary end. Raphael rejoices, too, over God's great gift of sexuality to the angels. Companionship rather than procreation dominates the view of marriage in the divorce tracts. I do not see how the same man could classify sexuality as a "secondary end" in *DCC* and also create the sexual speeches and scenes that he included in *Paradise Lost* (for what would Paradise be without sex?).

Chapter Nine

Milton's Own Possible Testimony

One of the most important pieces of evidence favoring Milton's authorship of *DDC* is an appendix that he added to the last edition of his *Defense of the English People*. It appeared in October 1658, just at the time when scholars have thought he was actively engaged with the treatise. In this conclusion to a work he clearly considered his masterpiece to date, he proudly proclaimed his accomplishments in it and stated that he was

> earnestly seeking how best I may show not only my own country ... but men of every land and, particularly, all Christian men, that for their sake I am at this time hoping and planning still greater things, if these be possible for me, as with God's help they will. (4.1.537)[1]

This certainly can be interpreted as a public statement of his current occupation with just such a work as *DDC* ("still greater things"), and his address (to "all Christian men") is similar to that of its opening words: "To All the Churches of Christ and to All in any part of the world who profess the Christian Faith" (6.117). So a leading authority, Cedric Brown, takes it: Milton promised "a major service to reformed religion, just as the Defense had been to political discourse."[2]

But another important scholar has related Milton's self-imposed program to another project: Masson judged that he was referring in these words to *Paradise Lost*,[3] which also was certainly well under way at just this time and which fits the Appendix description quite as well as the treatise. In favor of the idea that this section refers to the poem, one may note that in the *Defense* passage Milton states that to be successful he must rely on divine support if he is to accomplish anything, just as he does in *Paradise Lost*. Personal dependence upon divine guidance is absent from the Epistle of the treatise and indeed from the rest of its text. One may understand the promise to refer to work on the treatise, but such evidence is not decisive.

The next year Milton concluded *Of Civil Power* with another promise to his readers that he might write about "these things perhaps more some other time" (7.271). Some might understand this to mean that Milton was contemplating the expansion of the arguments of his tract in the larger compass of *DDC*. But the sentence reads better merely as the conclusion to the work. The tract had steadfastly opposed the intrusion of civil power into ecclesiastical matters;

it was not limited to questioning the authority of Old Testament laws for Christians, that narrow context within which *DDC* considers the issue (6.598–600).[4]

As a matter of fact, Milton himself states in these closing sentences how the argument should be amplified elsewhere: having considered it already "sufficiently out of the scriptures" in *Of Civil Power*, he seeks now further support from "testimonies, examples, experiences of all succeeding ages to these times asserting this doctrine" (7.272). But such social and historical perspective is exactly what the statement in *DDC* fails to provide. Rather, it argues only, as usual, from scriptural evidence (but relying upon different proof texts from Milton's). Milton does provide historical perspective for the subject, with relatively little scriptural evidence, on one aspect of the control of the church by magistrates—the legal collection of tithes, which is the issue considered in *Hirelings*. This sequel appeared a few months after *Of Civil Power*. Its opening sentence refers to his treatment of civil power in the earlier tract and then goes on to a second source of church corruption, "hire," that harms its ministers (7.277). The approach is historical rather than textual, matching the promise that Milton had made in his earlier tract. Thus the proposal made at the conclusion to *Of Civil Power* seems much more likely to anticipate *Hirelings* than *DDC*.

A third and very important statement supporting Milton's responsibility for the treatise is its extensive argument for divorce in book 1, chapter 10, which Barbara Lewalski has pointed to because of its harmony with the ideas in Milton's canonical divorce tracts.⁵ The treatise argues for divorce by advancing a much broader meaning of fornication than the word usually carries:

> as Selden demonstrated particularly well in his *Uxor Hebraea*, with the help of numerous Rabbinical texts, the word *fornication*, if it is considered in the light of the idiom of oriental languages, does not mean only adultery. It can mean also either what is called *some shameful thing* (i.e., the lack of some quality which might reasonably be required in a wife), Deut. xxiv.1, or it can signify anything which is found to be persistently at variance with love, fidelity, help and society (i.e. with the original institution of marriage). I have proved this elsewhere, basing my argument on several scriptural texts, and Selden has demonstrated the same thing. (6.378)

In this passage its author asserts that he has "found out" or "ascertained elsewhere" this interpretation ("ut nos alias . . . reperitur," p. 170),⁶ which is a much more generalized meaning of the word "fornication" as discussed in Deuteronomy 24.1 than that usually given it.

Kelley's note to the sentence convincingly cites *Tetrachordon* (2.673) as the work to which the author is referring. It adds to the authority of Deuteronomy that of Judges 19.2, a verse *DDC* also quotes as "the best text to demonstrate" this broader meaning.

If, as seems likely, this is the reference intended, it is the sole allusion in the treatise to any other work of Milton's. The text here correctly cites on the same subject his friend John Selden's *Uxor Hebraea*. Milton had developed such an interpretation even earlier in *Doctrine and Discipline* (2.335), where he traces such a reading to Hugo Grotius. He could not, of course, call on Selden's authority in either of these divorce tracts because the latter's *Uxor Hebraea*,[7] which the treatise cites, would not appear until 1646. Here in *DDC*, if Milton is the author, he traces his original interpretation of these biblical texts in the divorce tracts and adds Selden's later corroboration, of which he assuredly knew, for he referred to the *Uxor* by name in *Hirelings*.

As has been noted, Milton seems to have discussed this broader meaning of fornication after 1658 with his friend, former student, and "anonymous" biographer Cyriack Skinner; for Cyriack remembered this wider definition, associating it with both *Tetrachordon* and Selden's *Uxor Hebraea*: in that divorce tract he reported that Milton developed "another Sense of the word Fornication (and wch is also the Opinion amongst others of Mr. Selden in his *Uxor Hebraea*) then what is commonly received."[8] This is very close to the words actually printed above from *DDC*, and I think that similarity strongly implies direct access to their author—but after 1656, not in 1644 when Cyriack was one of Milton's students and when *Tetrachordon* appeared, two years before Selden would publish his book. As I have noted, it is the sole reference in the biography to a specific passage in *DDC*. I conclude that Milton himself or the amanuensis for the treatise—Jeremie Picard, whom Cyriack must have known—mentioned to the biographer this activity on Milton's part in relation to the treatise. From this information Cyriack could have drawn the implication that he was responsible for the entire work.

Besides Kelley's notes to this section, which argue a common authorship in parallels with Milton's tracts, especially with *Tetrachordon*, equally important to recognize is the fact that very few authors then dared touch this dangerous subject. One can find plenty of Socinians and Arminians who would agree with various irregularities of doctrine in *DDC*, but "divorcers" were a rare breed. I have tried without success to match this section of the work with that of someone else who wrote on divorce. Milton's name alone remains despite my best efforts to attach the passage to another author.

But in *DDC* this is an irregularly constructed chapter. As John Shawcross has observed in a private communication to me, its several digressions are "totally out of place in the treatise [because they become] argument, not theological discussion," and are "not concerned with explanation of ideas using proof texts as support to back up the theological position"; these parts are "simply incoherent with the beginning of the chapter and the rest of the treatise."

Before surrendering my argument against Milton's responsibility for *DDC* on the limited evidence of his projected responsibility for these few exceptional pages in chapter 10, I want to present an alternative hypothesis: Milton indeed may have dictated those pages on divorce, but they were then inserted after the passage on marriage that the author of the whole work had already set down. The primary evidence for such disjunction rests upon two Latin words for marriage.

Consider the following facts. In chapter 10 the subject of marriage is treated from page 120, line 5, to page 122, line 6; and again from 150, line 19, to 154, line 21. (I shall take up later the topic of polygamy, which seriously interrupts the discussion of marriage here between pages 122 and 150.) Then the subject of divorce immediately follows, extending from page 154, line 22, to 178, line 14, where the chapter ends. I am concerned with the different Latin words for marriage, *coniugium* and *matrimonium*, used in these pages. To my knowledge they are synonyms available by choice to an author.

In the pages on marriage, which I think are by the yet-unidentified author of *DDC*, I count two examples of *coniugium* or its derivatives on page 120, one on 150; then five on 152 and eight on 154—a total of 16. In addition, *coniugium* appears in the title of the chapter. There is not a single example of *matrimonium* in this entire section.

But in the pages on divorce, which we may assign to Milton, *matrimonium* appears four times on page 156, twice on pages 166, 170 and 174, four times on 176 , and once on 178—a total of 15 examples. He was, however, not averse to using *coniugium* freely, too: twice on page 154, five times on 156, once each on pages 164, 166 and 174, twice on 170 and 172, and three times on 176—a total of 17 examples, though the 5 on page 156 depend on the verb *coniunxit* of the Bible verse under discussion. I conclude that we are distinguishing the active vocabularies of two different authors. Milton indeed could have dictated the section on divorce, and someone appended it to the discussion of marriage already written by the author of the rest of the treatise. Milton freely interchanged *coniugium* and *matrimonium*; the other wrote only *coniugium*. The reason for the variations in the language of the pages assigned to Milton clearly is stylistic: they involve no semantic issues. The author of the other paragraphs, though, was not interested in such niceties. Perhaps here we have an example of why some of Milton's contemporaries admired his Latin style.

Unfortunately, the manuscript itself can give no evidence. Chapter 10 is in the part copied by Daniel Skinner, and at this juncture it is seamless. One might think that the addition of about seven pages would show up in the pagination of the whole book, but Kelley states that "pagination was by chapter rather than consecutive through the whole document" (6:23). There would thus be no problem with the added pages, though the time and circumstances of their addition are certainly moot.

The section on polygamy (page 122, line 6, to 150, line 18) that interrupts the otherwise continuous original statement about marriage offers some evidence that the author of the pages on divorce (Milton, in my view) was responsible for it too. *Coniugium* appears four times, on pages 122, 124, 126 and 138; as does *matrimonium* four times, on pages 132 and 146 and twice on 144. Here also is the sole example of a third Latin synonym for marriage—*connubium*—on page 128. In view of the *DDC* author's unwillingness to employ *matrimonium* at all, I tend to assign this section also to the author of the pages on divorce, who used each word about equally.

Another pair of Latin synonyms—those for "husband," *vir* and *maritus*—may offer a second distinction between the texts of two different authors. One must beware here of the alternate and more common meaning of *vir* as "man," though the other meaning of "husband" is well established, too. In the few pages on marriage in chapter 10, *vir* or its derivatives appear three times and *maritus*, twice. But the latter pair are exceptional, both being required to contrast with *dominum* (page 120), with which *vir* has no stylistic affinity. I also omit a fourth example of *vir* (page 122), where it must contrast with *foemina*, for which *maritus* would not be suitable. The author of the pages on marriage, that is, has a clear preference for *vir* over *maritus* to mean "husband."

But the author of the pages on divorce uses both words indiscriminately, just as he does *coniugium* and *matrimonium*. I count five appearances of *maritus* in this part of the chapter and two, possibly three, of *vir* (the one on page 162 may be limited to meaning "man"). Although the contrasting appearance of these two words in these two parts of the chapter is admittedly skimpy evidence, the differences squarely support the more convincing ones for "marriage."

Turning again to the argument for polygamy that so interrupts the statement about marriage, I find the same double usage for "husband" that governs the pages on divorce. *Vir* appears four times (I omit, because the word carries its other sense of "man," those on pages 122, 126 and 148, and three on 150). *Maritus* also appears four times, confirming the balance of *coniugium* and *matrimonium* already noted in this section on polygamy.⁹

The best way to account for such verbal contrasts between the section on marriage and those on polygamy and divorce is that the latter were inserted into an already existing text, perhaps by Skinner as he added them to this part of the treatise, though of course they may have already been present from an earlier time. But added they certainly were, for both are intrusive into their contexts. First, as has been observed, the section on polygamy breaks up an otherwise continuous statement about marriage. Second, both additions are far longer than the text into which they are incorporated, and there is no justification for their presence in its title, "Of the Special Government of Man before the Fall, Including the Institution of the Sabbath and of Marriage [*coniugio*]." Indeed, to consider polygamy and divorce as subjects to be instituted for mankind before the Fall is simply absurd. As John Shawcross has written,

> Chapter X was supposed to discuss the special government of man before the Fall, and to this was added, according to the title, the Sabbath and marriage. The treatise discusses these things in a [suitable] style and brevity. . . . But then comes the prolix discussion [of divorce], the same kind of prolixity and special pleading that Milton exhibited in *Tetrachordon*.¹⁰

Much later in the treatise, book 2 returns briefly to the subject. In his discussion of prudence, the author observes that prudence "is, as it were, a seasoning to be added to every virtue, as salt was to every sacrifice, leading to the maxim: *of the evils of sin, none is to be chosen.*" Following this dictum, he concludes that "some scholars" falsely interpret "the law. These scholars consider that usury, divorce, polygamy and so on were allowed to the Jews as being only venial sins," to which he protests that law cannot "concede or tolerate even the smallest of vices" (6.651), that is, exceptions. Kelley interprets this statement as an extension of the views of chapter 10 discussed above. It is proof, he observes, that, because it is "in Picard's hand, [it] indicates that Milton's belief in the lawfulness of polygamy was present in the last Picard draft" replaced by Skinner's copy and thus "was not a later addition to the manuscript" (n. 7)—an interesting interpretation, in its prescience rebutting just the argument that I have presented here (and incidentally proving that Kelley too recognized the material's intrusive nature). In response, I think that the author of the treatise was not asserting the legality of usury, divorce, and polygamy as such, but was pointing to them as examples to prove that laws do not indulge "venial" exceptions to themselves but are absolute principles. Some pettifoggers, today not identifiable, have thought that all laws are universal, affecting everyone equally at all times. They were forced, however, to recognize that the Old Testament certainly permitted usury, divorce, and polygamy—a fact for which they accounted by discounting them as being permitted because they are only "venial" sins. The author of the treatise will have none of this: a sin is a sin. He is not supporting these three exceptions but attacking the legal absolutism that rationalized their inclusion.

A final piece of evidence for a composite manuscript is a repetition that is hard to explain as the work of a single author. On page 154, *DDC* states that the "forma" of marriage "mutua coniugum, benevolentia, amore, auxilio, solatio consistet." But only 24 lines later it repeats that the "forma ipsa" of marriage "benevolentia . . ., amor, auxilium, solatium . . . constet" (page 156), unaccountably and needlessly repeating word for word the definition of marriage. One must note, however, that the first occurs near the conclusion of the discussion of marriage and the second in the other author's opening statement on divorce. There is no repetition, that is, but two independent texts. Nor is one copying from the other: both derive from a common antecedent, John Wolleb's *Compendium Christianae*, as Kelley has shown (6.370, n. 50): *"Forma coniugii in mutua coniugum benevolentia amore, auxilio, solatio, consistet."*

I cannot judge from my evidence whether the antisabbatarian arguments of chapter 10 were also an addition. I can conclude that Milton was probably responsible for the discussion of divorce in *DDC* as well as for the argument favoring polygamy. He or his amanuensis would have been recently occupied with the additions his friend and biographer Cyriack Skinner heard mentioned, and Skinner remembered at least one phrase from them. These additions were made, however, to an already existing manuscript of work written by someone else who used a somewhat different Latin vocabulary. Clearly one may not argue from his responsibility for these intrusive pages on polygamy and divorce that Milton was responsible for all the rest of the treatise. Its ideas diverge on many occasions too radically from those of the canonical works for this to be true.

The inconclusive evidence that has been cited from the 1658 Appendix to the *First Defense* and the apparent insertion of the passages concerning polygamy and divorce into an already completed statement about marriage do suggest, however, that Milton was at some time and to some degree engaged with the manuscript. We know that in 1658, when Jeremie Picard, the amanuensis, was associated with him, Milton was beginning to reactivate earlier projects. Thus about this time Edward Phillips reports that his uncle began to work again on *Paradise Lost* as well as on his *History of England* and the Latin thesaurus.[11] In 1658 he published "Sir Walter Ralegh's" *Cabinet Council*, a manuscript that he seems to have possessed for some time. The next year saw the appearance of *Hirelings*, which probably dates in some form back to 1653. Such renewed activity may also account for interlineations in the text of *DDC* that has come down to us: an underlying matrix for which he felt responsible because its author could no longer work on it, with many brief corrections and at least one overlay that Milton added with the paragraphs favoring divorce. Perhaps there are others, such as the inconsistent treatment of the date of the creation of the angels, discussed in chapter 8 of this book.

A work that Milton published over his name in 1672 is the *Artis Logicae*, which consists mostly of his extended overlays upon the matrices provided by the works of Peter Ramus and of his English interpreter at Christ's College, George Downame. Like *DDC* it is in Latin, though not addressed so narrowly to a Continental audience as the religious work (its first pages, for example, mention Sir Philip Sidney and Sir Francis Bacon). A somewhat analogous reworking of another's text can explain some of the anomalies that the treatise presents.[12] Whether he would have published it as his own, as he did the *Logic*, is anybody's guess, though one hopes not. Nor can one determine today, as Campbell, et al., agree, just which eccentric arguments he would have let stand. He compressed the last four chapters of Ramus's *Dialecticae* into one, perhaps wishing to have the same number of chapters in books 1 and 2 of both works, 33 and 17, though the significance of this correspondence is not clear (8.390, n. 1). If one accepts this thesis of an earlier text of *DDC* to which Milton has added his own longer comments on at least one occasion and perhaps others (together with the multitude of minor changes that Kelley has observed in the Picard parts of the manuscript), it seems impossible to ascertain now who authored the original matrix or the exact extent of Milton's overlay. The most plausible provenance is that the author was a friend of Milton, probably a former student, who died or for some other reason could not complete it.

Chapter Ten

Conclusions

There is no doubt that when Milton died in November 1674 he had in his possession the copy of *DDC* that survives today in London's Public Record Office. There is no reason to question that an acquaintance named Jeremie Picard had copied it from an earlier draft and did so before he entered, possibly at blind Milton's direction, a multitude of minor additions and changes. These would have been made before May 1660, when Picard disappears from record of any further association with Milton, perhaps because of the great disruptions to Milton's life attendant upon the Restoration of the Monarchy at the end of that month. Because Picard must have required many months to reproduce the whole extended and complex text before he entered any of these additions to it, he must have begun his transcription long before. Early 1658 seems too late for him or anyone else to have begun the original which he would copy. As for an earliest date, at least some work on this postulated original form must have been done after 1651, the latest year that I can identify for publication of any work that it cites.

To repeat, we do not know who wrote that original text that Picard copied. The common assumption has been that it was Milton himself, whom his biographer, nephew, and student Edward Phillips has recorded as apparently having had his students write "from his own dictation" such a work. Examination of the contents of the treatise makes this highly unlikely. A major factor is the elementary nature of the primary text by Wolleb underlying it, not at all suited to Milton's intellectual level then. Another student and biographer, Cyriack Skinner, recorded Milton's involvement with such a work, even quoting almost verbatim a sentence from it that occurs in a long and digressive insertion on divorce that indeed could have been by Milton, though it occurs in the context of the work of someone else. Cyriack's further knowledge of the contents of the treatise upon which he assumed Milton was occupied shows him to be so distant that it is with only questionable authority that he can report who was responsible for the rest of it. Finally, it is unlikely that the newly graduated Daniel Skinner, who actually would possess the manuscript and upon whose information, except for Edward Phillips's, the early biographers ultimately depend, knew Milton well enough before the poet's death to testify accurately to its true provenance. There is thus no finally conclusive proof of Milton's authorship in any of their surviving work.

Rather, the evidence (if the original manuscript—not its copy made by Picard—is indeed to be associated at all with Milton) points to one of his students as author, for whom such an outline of doctrine provided by Wolleb's *Compendium*, to which he added his own comments and biblical proof texts, would be a good scholastic exercise. It is based upon conservative Calvinism. But then overlaying much of this original are extended arguments originating from inspiration by the "Spirit" rather than reflection upon the "Letter" of the Bible and supporting highly eccentric doctrines. To identify their origin, it is necessary to recognize the authors to whom these additions respond. Without exception they are associated with the Continent, "our" writers always being located there, even the Englishman Ames. Every English dogmatist with whom Milton was familiar is totally ignored.

Bishop Burgess noted that there was no relationship between the authorities—both native and foreign—that Milton cited in the works we know are his and those important to the author of the treatise. A century and a half later Maurice Kelley repeated with even greater force exactly the same observations, though his purpose was certainly not that of the Bishop, to dissociate Milton from *DDC*.

A means of accounting for this perplexing state of affairs is to postulate that one of Milton's students composed, at his direction, a summary of faith based on Wolleb and Ames which he took abroad and modified under the influence of liberal thinkers there. Most probably he was resident in the Low Countries and Saumur because these are the locations of the main authors to whose work he responded, either in support of his ideas or in disagreement. Because a copy of his text came into Milton's possession, this former student may have brought it back and Picard copied it. But who he was we have no way to know. Whoever he was, he appears not to have published anything and was not interested in the practical problems of a parish (he shows little real concern for its subject in book 2, which focuses on "Works"), and, indeed, with his beliefs he could not have been ordained. Nor was he interested in law or politics. His real concern was theology, in which he would have had great difficulty establishing himself because of his eccentric views.

Picard himself is an attractive possibility, perhaps being the "Mr. Packer" who was remembered as one of Milton's students. But the name *Picard* adds nothing to our knowledge because we know so little about him. The name is common in the Low Countries, where there is the region of Picardy. His disappearance from the Milton records may have arisen from incipient insanity, for a man with a similar name identified as a former amanuensis of Milton was mentioned as being treated in London's hospital for the insane. Such a reason (or death) can explain why Milton cared enough for his work that he preserved it, probably used some of its ideas and even its proof texts for his own purposes, and added to it what he considered an occasional minor improvement. The manuscript reveals no major alterations that must be attributed to him unless they are the paragraphs on polygamy and divorce, though of course there may be other shorter ones like those concerned with the date of the creation of heaven and the angels. He did rework and publish over his own name the logic of George Downham, whose nephew and namesake he certainly knew as a fellow student in Christ's College; there would be no outcry over its Ramism. Some similar goal may have been his plan for *DDC*.

In its case, however, so many of Milton's genuine ideas are at odds with those in *DDC* that he could not have been its author unless he were the most incoherent thinker in history. He proves dogmas by quite different biblical texts from those cited for the same points in the treatise. His view of the Trinity is sharply different, as is that of the Incarnation, of the inspired reading of the Bible, of what constitutes heresy, of predestination, of the materiality of God, and of several other topics. It seems clear that one can use the treatise to interpret any of Milton's pertinent ideas, just as one can apply any other contemporary document to them. But it is dangerous to develop as "Milton's" any arguments found only in it and not supported by the canonical writings. The history of modern Milton scholarship abounds with such pitfalls. Many eccentric theories explored as his find sole or major support from *DDC* alone. Examples (analyses of which have often added new words to our vocabularies and to which I myself have contributed) include chiliasm, monophysitism, mystical theopantism, the theopaschite heresy, and the theopathetic tradition.[1]

The innovative and convincing stylometric study

made by Campbell, et al., offers a partial confirmation of these conclusions—confirmation based on analysis radically different from mine. These scholars have developed a new and original means of determining the authorship of a Latin text. (It is somewhat analogous to the method that has been used to determine, from their Greek originals, which of those letters tradition assigned to him St. Paul was really responsible for.) The procedure, possible only on a computer, discovers the 50 words that occur most frequently (and with what frequency) in a known text and then compares this list with the equivalent one derived from the text under question—in this case *DDC*.[2]

The authors first verified the reliability of this procedure by comparing known texts—the statistical results from Milton's three *Defenses* and ten representative contemporary Latin texts by such authors as Ames, Bacon, Salmasius and Wolleb. Plotting the results on a graph proves visually that the method is sound, as it convincingly distinguishes the fifty most frequently used words in each *Defense* (all of which group closely together and overlap frequently) from those of the other writers, and each of the latter from the others.

The authors then compare the frequency lists of the *Defenses* with those of *DDC*. The results appear in two clusters which, although they never overlap as do those of the *Defenses*, are in close association, especially impressive as compared with the more distant plottings of the texts from the other ten authors. This method, then, leads these authors to conclude that

Milton revised an earlier text (of uncertain origin); but because he stopped before completing the revision, we cannot now determine "what deletions of doctrines to which he did not subscribe" he might have made. In any case the stylometric evidence presented here underscores the similarity, but not identity, between Milton's acknowledged writings and the treatise even though, of course, it cannot remotely touch the problems of inconsistent theological dogmas between treatise and canon that I have argued at length.

The procedure does, however, raise one question. The graphs clearly show the close clustering of the words in all three *Defenses* and the somewhat looser clustering of those in *DDC*; but, surprisingly, though they are in the same general area of the graph, they never overlap, as one would expect to occur at least occasionally from a single author in writings confined to a single decade and that do occur among the *Defenses*. The explanation that Campbell, et al., offer for this separation is that "there would appear to be a split between the genres under consideration"— the political polemics of the *Defenses* versus the theology of the treatise accounting for the observed differences. But if the analysis is sound, such a large sampling of the 50 most frequently used words should mostly discount genres. Even if in one text, because of its subject, a word like "deus" should appear with exceptional frequency, most of the other 49 should not be affected by genre alone. Indeed, most of the 50 will be commonplace differences found in examples like "et" and "atque," or "nec" and "neque" and so on—structural words not responsive to different subjects. One should not, however, ignore the observation that the *Defenses* graph not far from *DDC* whereas both groups are clearly separated from the ten controls. Some kind of significant relationship clearly obtains between the clusters of the *Defenses* and those of the treatise, even though they never overlap as one would expect them to.

I think that this fact supports the thesis that I have proposed on quite different grounds: that one of Milton's former students was responsible for most of the text of *DDC*. The most frequently used words are exactly those structural ones that a student will pick up from his instructor and imitate in writing a foreign language. Both the separation of the two clusters and their relative closeness can, I think, be best understood in view of this thesis of composition by a former student who writes similarly to but not exactly like his master. I find, that is, that the similarities so clearly distinguished by Campbell's statistical methods are independent but strong support for my own hypothesis of how the work originated. They give special consideration to the Preface as being perhaps more "Miltonic" than the rest of the work, a conclusion Lewalski also reached.[3] This is, of course, quite possible, though I question whether the preface is long enough to provide an adequate sampling of the vocabulary; it graphs closer to the *Defenses* than does the rest of the treatise, but again is not within their perimeter. I repeat that the understanding of heresy presented in it is quite different from Milton's.

In conclusion I turn once again to the biographical

fact that in the parish of St. Giles, Cripplegate, there is no evidence that anyone thought of Milton as a heretic. Although some argue that he wanted his "dearest and best possession," the ideas in the treatise, to enlighten the whole Christian world, he was unaccountably silent about them in his little universe of Artillery Walk, keeping them from his neighbors and thus from his parish priest, whom they would certainly have shocked. For then Milton could never have been buried in its church according to the form prescribed by its Book of Common Prayer.

Notes

Notes to Introduction

1. Arthur Sewell, *A Study in Milton's Christian Doctrine*, 81–82.
2. John Rumrich, "Milton's God and the Matter of Chaos," 1038.
3. See Barbara Lewalski, "Forum," 144.
4. A similar motive must lie back of earlier reprints of Milton's pamphlet in 1809 and 1811.
5. In James Ogden's "Bishop Burgess and John Milton." He appends a list of books with important Milton associations that the library holds.
6. This suggestion, which I originally made in Vancouver, has been met to a considerable extent by Campbell, et al., in *Milton and De Doctrina Christiana*. Anyone concerned with the issues that follow must consult this important study. I am in substantial agreement with their conclusions.

Notes to Chapter One

1. Helen Darbishire, *Early Lives of Milton*, 5.
2. For a delightful and authoritative guide to the building and Milton's burial there, see Sister M. Christopher Pecheux, *Milton: A Topographical Guide*, 84–95.
3. See Allen Walker Read's interesting account, "The Disinterment of Milton's Remains," for details and Michael Lieb's analysis, *Milton and Violence*, 3–8.
4. There is a tradition reported by one early biographer that "in the latter part of his Life, he was not a profest Member of any particular Sect among Christians, he frequented none of their Assemblies, nor made use of their peculiar Rites in his Family" (John Toland, whose

religious biases may make him here an unreliable chronicler, in Darbishire, 195. The mention of "sect" and of "peculiar rites" implies absence from Puritan rather than Anglican services.) Milton's household deposed in the hearing over the disposition of his estate that they were "greate frequenters of the Church," which must have been Anglican. J. Milton French, *Life Records*, 5.211.

5. Christopher Hill, *Milton and the English Revolution*. Unhappily, as some reviewers observed, Hill could offer no proof of the existence of the local political groups he postulates, but surely Milton enjoyed some kind of social life with friends in the St. Giles parish.

6. As Nathaniel Henry has observed, "The environmental and intellectual influences of the Church of England were pervasive in his life and work." See his carefully argued essay "John Milton, Anglican" for details.

7. The Prayerbook's words in turn derive from Psalms 148 and 150. I have shown in "Herbert and Milton" how in his early years Milton fit within the Anglican pattern until Archbishop Laud began to enforce a narrow high-church conformity. Even then he opposed the governing structure of the church, not its dogmatic teachings.

8. In the six temptations that follow, Jesus obeys twice each of these three baptismal warnings: three affecting the divine nature, derived from Luke, and three parallel but original ones affecting the human nature. See my "The Double Set of Temptations in *Paradise Regained*."

9. Daniel Doerksen, "Milton and the Jacobean Church of England." This instructive essay shows that one could in Milton's day occupy in many respects a middle ground between Puritan and Anglican. Bishop Burgess had also noted this identification with the Church of England. *Milton Not the Author*, 204.

10. Details are conveniently available in French, *Life Records of John Milton*, 5.211–24.

11. Darbishire, 4.

12. A good brief survey of this aspect of the history of the manuscript that follows is in Maurice Kelley's Introduction to *DDC* (6.36–40). The details are exhaustively reproduced in Campbell, et al., pp. 67–89.

13. See Herman Scherpbier *Milton in Holland*, 63. This information derives from a statement made many years later by Limborch to Zacharias von Uffenbach, who reported it in his *Merkwürdige Reisen* (1754). See Campbell, et al., for a full account. There seems to be no reason to question the story.

Notes to Chapter Two

1. Darbishire reprints all of them. Pertinent pages are for Aubrey, pp. 9–10; the Anonymous Biographer, 29, 31; Wood, 46, 47; Phillips, 61; Toland, 192; and Richardson, 268. Subsequent citations are by page in the text. In error she assigned the authorship of the Anonymous Biography to Milton's other nephew, John Phillips.

2. William R. Parker, *Milton: A Biography*, 1.14 and 2.881. Peter Beal has recently confirmed this identification.

3. See Parker's note, 2.900–01.

4. See French, *Life Records*, 4.317–18.

5. *Of Education* likewise prescribes that students spend "Sundayes . . . in the highest matters of *Theology*" (2.399).

6. I have used the translation by Eusden. One should also consult Keith Sprunger's biography, *The Learned Dr. William Ames*.

7. Conveniently accessible as translated by John W. Beardslee.

8. Kelley himself made this point in "Milton's Debt to Wolleb's *Compendium Theologiae Christianae*," which later he would strengthen as "too carefully understat[ing] Wolleb's contribution" (6.18, n. 15).

9. John D. Eusden recognizes the *Medulla* "not as a scholarly treatise but as a useful compendium for laymen and students" (Ames, *Medulla Theologica*, 2).

Notes to Chapter Three

1. Kelley has made a careful study of these matters in his edition of *DDC* (6.23–38).

2. Kelley (6.23, n. 4).

3. James Holly Hanford, "The Rosenbach Milton Documents." See further Campbell, et al., pp. 89–91.

4. Samuel Leigh Sotheby, *Ramblings*, 95.

5. See Shawcross's entry, "Amanuenses," in *A Milton Encyclopedia*, 1.42–43. All these matters have been meticulously reviewed and documented by Campbell, et al. Picard finished copying the entire manuscript before the Restoration, for as Parker pointed out (2.1057), it comments near the end on how church authority is exercised "as bishops once did and as many magistrates do nowadays" (6.805). Besides providing a firm date before which the copy was completed, this may be the only identifiable reference in the work to contemporary events in England. It interrupts a long collection of proof texts, suggesting that it was a late addition made before Picard had completed his copy of the original manuscript.

Although all the evidence of Picard's association with Milton is limited to the years 1658 to 1660, this fact cannot deny that these relations may have begun at an earlier or ended at a later time.

6. "New Light on Milton's Amanuensis," 383–84. Again Campbell, et al., provide full details, pp. 90–91.

7. See the details of my inquiries in "Ramblings."

8. See Leo Miller, *John Milton's Writings in the Anglo-Dutch Negotiations, 1651–1654*.

9. See Parker's biography, 2.1008.

10. In Kelley's *This Great Argument*, conclusions somewhat qualified by Campbell, et al., pp. 93–97.

11. *This Great Argument*, 41.

12. Kelley, 42–56 and 227–56. See my summary in "Ramblings," 44–45.

13. Again the best authority to consult is Campbell, et al., pp. 91–93.

14. Information conveniently summarized in Parker, 1.610–11, and 2.1130–32, though he accepts far too readily a close association of Milton and Skinner well before the former's death for which there is no evidence at all.

15. Samuel Pepys, *Letters and the Second Diary*, 60.

16. David Masson, *Life of John Milton*, 6.791; and Parker, 2.1131, n. 19.

17. In writing to Pepys, he lied about the location of the two manuscripts. Another letter to Pepys French judged to "contain a veiled hint of blackmail": "'That Late Villain Milton'" 103. He did not repay as promised £10 he owed the diarist. Kelley remarks on his "manifest untrustworthiness" (6.37).

18. French, "'That Late Villain Milton,'" 103.

19. Parker, 1.611.

20. Robert Fallon, *Milton in Government*, 226.

21. French, *Life Records*, 5.238.

22. Fallon, 221, n. 3, and 225.

23. Masson, 6.794.

24. Shawcross, *Milton: A Bibliography for the Years 1624–1700*, item 319. Milton's texts of the State Papers seem to have been quite accessible. Someone made an early transcription, now in the Columbia University Library. Besides the one on which *Literae* is based and Skinner's, Shawcross has traced two others: one reproduced in Gregorio Leti's *Historia* (Amsterdam, 1692) and one in John Lünig's *Literae Procerum Europae* (Leipzig, 1712), in Shawcross, *Achievements*, 354–58, the information about the Leipzig publication deriving from Miller, "Milton's State Letters," 412–14.

25. Burgess, *Milton not the Author*, 14, although as he recognized, this "clean" copy has itself many corrections and errors. We do not know, however, how corrupt was the text from which he worked.

26. Charles Sumner thought Milton himself dictated the word because the work was to appear after his death.

27. See my "Provenance" for reproductions of all three and the supporting arguments of Campbell, et al., pp. 91–93.

28. Thomas Burgess's preface to *Protestant Union*, which introduces his reprint of Milton's *Of True Religion*.

29. Burgess, *Milton Not the Author*, 75.

30. These documents still survive with the manuscript, catalogued as SP 9/61. Significantly, Lemon did not offer the prefixed names to authenticate his discovery.

31. *Protestant Union*, xlviii.

Notes to Chapter Four

1. Christopher Hill, "Hunter, Burgess, and Milton." Rumrich, for example, in *Milton Unbound* judges this essay to be a "devastating rebuttal," 154, n. 39. On mortalism, as

Anthony Low penetratingly observes in a yet-unpublished essay, "Milton and the Soul," "Whatever Adam tells himself in this soliloquy must be understood in its dramatic context," which is "ratiocination without benefit of any reliable foundation and without the possession of any certain knowledge of the future—especially knowledge of the Redemption. The soliloquy consists of a bewildered circling from one theoretical point to the next, and resembles nothing so much as the philosophical debates among the fallen angels in Hell." Thus one may not conclude from Adam's words that Milton himself was a mortalist or not. He never alludes to the idea elsewhere.

2. 178.

3. See Kelley's useful textual appendix to page 598 (page 411 of the manuscript) at 6.830.

4. See my "Milton and the Waldensians."

5. Lewalski, "Forum," 144.

6. Burgess, *Milton Not the Author*, p. 62.

7. Burgess, 63.

8. Samuel Schoenbaum, *William Shakespeare: A Documentary Life* 192, 193. But Campbell, et al., p. 98, report a different practice during the Interregnum. Parliament "charged the civil magistrate with the responsibility of using the apparatuses at his disposal to effect collection. This became, in effect, a new way for the civil magistrate to be involved in matters of religious practice or belief. . . . At the Restoration, ecclesiastical courts were eventually resurrected, and the failure to pay tithes fell [again] within their sphere of judgment; from 1661 the matter became once more outside the range of the civil magistrate.

"The discussion of the issue in [*DDC*] would be wholly congruent if the treatise were written before the Restoration and if this passage had escaped late revision in the light of the renovation of the ecclesiastical courts. It is in no sense pertinent that Milton does not make this argument or attack this phenomenon in *Hirelings*, which is a pamphlet explicitly addressed to Parliament." But Milton's point seems to me to be the activity of the "wolvish ministers" who institute the suits rather than the courts in which they were tried.

Notes to Chapter Five

1. Burgess, *Milton Not the Author*, 66. I had independently reached the same conclusion in "The Provenance of the *Christian Doctrine*," 131–32, and even earlier in the perplexities of reconciliation that I had tried to overcome in "The Theological Context of the *Christian Doctrine*" (1976).

2. See *Confession*, Article 24.6: "The corruption of man [is] such as is apt to study arguments, unduly to put aside those whom God hath joined in marriage." In England in 1647 with the recent publication of his divorce tracts so clearly in everyone's mind, the public meaning had to be "the corruption of John Milton is such as to study these arguments." A silent Milton in *DDC* under such circumstances is difficult to imagine. The clause was removed in the Savoy Declaration of 1658, which modified some articles of the *Confession*.

3. Paul Stanwood, "Of Prelacy and Polity," 66.

4. Burgess, 25.

5. Burgess, 61.

6. H.J. Todd, *Some Account of the Life and Writings of John Milton*, 360.

7. Turner, 345.

8. Harris Fletcher, *The Use of the Bible*, 86–88.

9. Burgess, 30–31. For the complexities of the two

traditions of this text Paul Sellin has called my attention to the remarkable study of New Testament variants being undertaken by Reuben J. Swanson. See his Prolegomena to Matthew.

10. Burgess, 60.

11. J.P. Pittion, "Milton, La Place, and Socinianism," 139.

12. Pittion quotes a number of similar but not exact parallels.

13. Brian G. Armstrong, *Calvinism and the Amyraut Heresy*, 124.

14. Armstrong, 115.

15. For extended treatment of the major conflict among the French Huguenots see Armstrong's study of the Amyraut heresy and F.P. van Stam's *The Controversy over the Theology of Savmur, 1635-1650*. Recently in "John Milton's *Paradise Lost* and *De Doctrina Christiana*," Paul Sellin demonstrates how different is Milton's interpretation of predestination from that argued in *DDC*. This incisive essay also clearly distances Milton from the Arminianism with which he has been charged on the basis of the treatise, an insight never noted before.

16. van Stam, 15.

17. I have not been able to locate any list of the members of its student body.

Notes to Chapter Six

1. Lewalski, "Forum," 248-49.

2. Beardslee, *Reformed Dogmatics*, 30, 35.

3. Ames, *Medulla*, 63.

4. I have developed this approach in "The Theological Context of the *Christian Doctrine*."

5. Hill, "Hunter, Burgess, and Milton," 184.

6. Beardslee, 164-71.

7. In his discussion of justification, book 1, chapter 28, Ames cites some 50 proof texts but actually quotes only about a third of them. They are all within the text, not in the margins. See Eusden's translation, 160–64.

8. See my edition of *Hirelings* (7.278, n. 9, and 279, n. 10).

9. Hill thinks that there is such a parallel, "Hunter, Burgess, and Milton," 187, n. 35.

10. See my introduction to the edition of *Hirelings* (7.230, n. 6). I think however, that Milton's concern for the Waldensians whom it eloquently cites mostly dated after their "massacre" at Easter 1655.

Notes to Chapter Seven

1. Lewalski, "Forum," 150–52. As further evidence of Milton's responsibility for the treatise she cites a passage from *Paradise Lost* in which "in terms which recall *De Doctrina*, Milton has God himself deny predestination and insist that his conditional decrees guarantee human liberty." But in his "Milton's *Paradise Lost* and *De Doctrina*" Paul Sellin points out that the lines (3.112–22) that she quoted to prove this apply to fallen angels, not mankind (45–46). He goes on to demonstrate at length how poem and treatise diverge on this important subject.

2. Lewalski considers the problem in *Milton's Brief Epic*, 145–46.

3. Burgess, *Milton Not Milton*, note on page 9.

4. E.g., 7.264.

5. This is sharply at odds with *DDC*, which judges that "consubstantiation and particularly transubstantiation ... are utterly alien to common sense and human behavior. What is more, they are irreconcilable with sacred doctrine" (6.554).

6. A point supported in *DDC* (6.164–65), with which Milton is here disagreeing.

7. Nowhere in the canonical works does Milton support adult against infant baptism. The treatise argues strongly for it (6.544–52). It may be worth mention that the author of the treatise prefers *obsignatio* (seal) to *sacramentum* (sacrament). Thus his chapter 28 on the sacraments he titles "De Obsignatione Foederis Gratiae Externa": "Of the External Sealing of the Covenant of Grace." He freely uses both words but begins his discussion of baptism as "the first (seal), commonly called a sacrament": "primum . . . sacramentum vulgo dictum" (Columbia edition, 16.168). Later he adds that "a sacrament is nothing but a seal": "sacramentum nihil aliud nisi obsignatio" (204).

Milton never makes such an identification.

8. Polanus, *The Substance of Christian Religion*, 43; Ames, *Medulla Theologica*, (Amsterdam, 1623), Disputation Six, or Disputation Five in the Amsterdam, 1627, edition, the same as that of 1629, which was the last issued during Ames's lifetime and the one translated by Eusden, 89; Wolleb, *Compendium Theologiae Christianae* in Beardslee, 43; *Westminster Confession of Faith*, 2.3, and 8.2; and Cappel, *Syntagma Thesium Theologicarum*, part 1, 161. The last had been printed as early as 1641. There are similar sets of proof texts in the works of other Reformed dogmatists, but this is a representative selection.

9. As Stevie Davies and I have shown in "Milton's Urania."

10. Adamson and I advanced this evidence independently. See his essay, "Milton's Arianism" of 1960 and my own "The Meaning of 'Holy Light,'" of 1959. Both appear with some revisions in *Bright Essence*. In *The Sacred Complex* William Kerrigan disagrees, observing that the light of the Invocation to *Paradise Lost* book 3 "is expressly

differentiated from the Heavenly Muse of the first invocation, who 'taught' the poet to master the infernal realms of the first two books," 150. I fail to see why the poet may not have both physical and inward illumination in mind. He concludes his prayer by asking that "thou Celestial light [may]/Shine inward and the mind through all her powers/Irradiate" (3.51–53). Kerrigan goes on to point out that my "thesis must also get around the alternative of the opening lines, since the *Christian Doctrine* is emphatic on the createdness of the Son" as indeed it is. "Must we suppose that Milton changed his mind on the heresy most thoroughly argued in his [sic] text?" I confess that I have changed mine.

11. See my "The War in Heaven."

12. This is our common thesis in *Bright Essence*, underlying several of its essays. The term "subordination" makes some uncomfortable (e.g., most recently Rumrich, *Milton Unbound*, 42–44). They prefer "anti-Trinitarian." I have avoided the latter because it seems to me to deny all aspects of the Trinitarian Godhead, whereas the former more accurately questions only one of them.

13. Fallon also makes this point in *Divided Empire*, 162 ff. Underlying this conception is the doctrine of kenosis derived from Philippians 1.6–8.

14. These and other early questions of the orthodoxy of *Paradise Lost* are conveniently available in Shawcross, *Milton: The Critical Heritage* and *Milton 1732–1801: The Critical Heritage*.

15. H.R. MacCullum, "Milton and Figurative Interpretation."

16. See, for example, Madsen, *From Shadowy Types to Truth*.

17. Lewalski, "Forum," 152. Indeed, it has kept them busy for nearly a century.

18. See Thomas S.K. Scott-Craig, "The Craftsmanship and Theological Significance of Milton's *Art of Logic*" and Kelley's note on the passage in *DDC* (6.216, n. 37).

19. Burgess, Preface to *Protestant Union*, pp. xix–xx.

20. "The Symbol of Chalcedon," in Phillip Schaff, II, 62.

21. See my "Milton on the Incarnation."

22. Lewalski, "The Problem of Christ's Nature," in *Milton's Brief Epic*.

23. Schaff, 1.32.

Notes to Chapter Eight

1. J.H. Adamson's "Milton and the Creation" is reprinted in *Bright Essence*.

2. *Confessions*, 12.7.

3. Michael Lieb, *The Dialectics of Creation*, 16–17.

4. A.S.P. Woodhouse, "Notes on Milton's Views on the Creation," 229, n. 30.

5. Regina Schwartz, *Remembering and Creating: Biblical Creation in "Paradise Lost,"* 11. Recent developments in chaos theory and in investigating Milton's depiction of chaos in its light have enlisted the interest of several perceptive critics. See especially the essays by Mary F. Norton, Catherine Gimelli Martin and John P. Rumrich.

6. *Confessions*, 11.11.

7. Burton, *The Anatomy of Melancholy*, part 1, sect. 1, mem. 10, subsec. 2.

8. Burton, Subsec. 5.

9. Without wishing to argue the point further here, it seems to me that Raphael-Milton is consciously applying to the universe the monistic unification provided by neo-Platonism with the flowing out of being from "the One" to lower levels of existence and its subsequent return. D. Bentley Hart, in "Matter, Monism, and Narrative,"

18–19, questions Milton's employment here of this tradition.

10. Lewalski, "Forum," 149.

11. See my "The Power of Matter."

12. See Robert H. West, *Milton and the Angels* (Athens, GA, 1955).

13. This statement appears in the part of book 1, chapter 10 that I think was not dictated by Milton, a point I shall discuss in Chapter 9.

Notes to Chapter Nine

1. Milton, *Defense of the English People*. The original Latin is conveniently available too (4.ii.1138–39).

2. Cedric C. Brown, *John Milton: A Literary Life*, 144.

3. Masson, *Life*, 5.574.

4. I have considered earlier the concomitant issue of the authority of Old Testament law.

5. Lewalski, "Forum," p. 149.

6. To have access to the Latin text I refer by page here and in the next few paragraphs to volume 15 of *The Works of John Milton*, eds. James Holly Hanford and Waldo Hilary Dunn. It translates this phrase from page 170 as "shown," and Kelley as "proves" (6.378), both of which may imply publication. Paul Sellin convincingly questions these readings of the Latin in "The Reference to John Milton's *Tetrachordon* in *De Doctrina Christiana*."

7. The citations to Selden can be conveniently found in *John Selden on Jewish Marriage Law*, translated by Jonathan R. Ziskind, 406–21. See also Ziskind's discussion of divorce as it relates to Milton and his own day, Introduction, 24–27. In a private communication John Shawcross has pointed out to me that Selden's title actually is *Uxor Ebraica*. The *DDC* spelling repeats that of the *Second Defense*, dated May, 1654 (4.i.626, although the

translation and notes do not record this spelling) which also appears in the Anonymous Biography (Darbishire, 23) and which seems to be quoting, as I have pointed out, from the sentence in the treatise. "What this suggests," Shawcross continues, "is that the scribe of the Second Defense could have been the scribe of *DDC*—Picard?" He warns, however, that this variant does not necessarily support my argument that the treatise is not Milton's.

8. Darbishire, 23.
9. The stylometric study reported by Campbell, et al., confirms these conclusions.
10. Shawcross, "Forum," 161.
11. Darbishire, 72.
12. Campbell, et al., also reach this conclusion.

Notes to Conclusions

1. For chiliasm see Michael Fixler, *Milton and the Kingdoms of God*; for monophysitism, Lewalski, *Milton's Brief Epic*, 155–56; for mystical theopantism, Walter Clyde Curry, *Milton's Ontology Cosmogony, and Physics*, 43; for the theopaschite heresy, my "Milton on the Incarnation," 144; for the theopathetic tradition, Lieb, "Milton and the Theopathetic Tradition." I have briefly considered this last concept in the appendix to "Milton on the Passions," 87–88. Note also Dennis Danielson's unease over the disparity of the conception of theodicy between *DDC* and the rest of the canon in his stimulating book, *Milton's Good God*, especially page 157.

2. Campbell, et al., pp. 104–10 and accompanying graphs.

3. "Forum," 153, a conclusion with which Campbell, et al., "most certainly concur," p. 108, but which I cannot so assuredly accept, as the evidence I have presented shows.

Works Cited

Adamson, J.H. "Milton and the Creation." *Journal of English and Germanic Philology*, 61 (1962), 756–78. Reprinted in Hunter, et al., *Bright Essence*, 1971.

Ames, William. *Medulla Theologica* (1629), trans. John D. Eusden as *The Marrow of Divinity*. Boston: Pilgrim Press, 1968.

Armstrong, Brian G. *Calvinism and the Amyraut Heresy*. Madison, WI: University of Wisconsin Press, 1969.

Augustine, Saint. *The Confessions*, trans. R.S. Pine-Coffin. London: Penguin, 1961.

Beardslee, John W. *Reformed Dogmatics*. New York: Oxford University Press, 1965.

Brown, Cedric C. *John Milton: A Literary Life*. New York: Cambridge University Press, 1995.

Burgess, Thomas, Bishop of Salisbury. "Preface," *Protestant Union* (London, 1825), a reprint of Milton's *Of True Religion* (1673).

———. *Milton Not the Author of the Lately Discovered Arian Work De Doctrina Christiana. Three Discourses Delivered at the Anniversary Meetings of the Royal Society of Literature. In the Years 1826, 1827, and 1828. To Which Is Added, Milton Contrasted with Milton and with the Scriptures*. London, 1829.

Burton, Robert. *The Anatomy of Melancholy*. 3 vols. London: Dent, 1926.

Campbell, Gordon, Thomas N. Corns, John K. Hale, David Holmes, and Fiona Tweedie. *Milton and De Doctrina Christiana*. Published electronically 5 October 1996 and reprinted with a few changes in *Milton Quarterly*, 31 (October, 1997): 67–121 as "The Provenance of *De Doctrina Christiana*." See *The Milton Home Page* (Milton on the Web-Scholarly

Works Cited

Articles) from the University of Richmond (http://www.urich.edu/n creamer/miltonhtral).

Cappel, Joshua. *Syntagma Thesium Theologicorum in Academia Salmuriense.* Saumur, 1655.

Chalcedon, Creed of. See Schaff.

Curry, Walter Clyde. *Milton's Ontology, Cosmogony, and Physics.* Lexington, KY: University of Kentucky Press, 1957.

Danielson, Dennis. *Milton's Good God: A Study in Literary Theodicy.* Cambridge, U.K.: Cambridge University Press, 1982.

Darbishire, Helen. *Early Lives of Milton.* London: Constable, 1932.

Doerksen, Daniel. "Milton and the Jacobean Church of England." *Early Modern Literary Studies*, 1 (1995): 1–23.

Elton, William. "New Light on Milton's Amanuenses." *Huntington Library Quarterly*, 26 (1963): 383–84.

Fallon, Robert. *Milton in Government*, University Park, PA: Pennsylvania State University Press, 1993.

———. *Divided Empire.* University Park, PA: Pennsylvania State University Press, 1995.

Fixler, Michael. *Milton and the Kingdoms of God.* Evanston, IL: Northwestern University Press, 1964.

Fletcher, Harris. *The Use of the Bible in Milton's Prose*, in *University of Illinois Studies in Language and Literature*, 14 (1929).

French, J. Milton. "'That Late Villain Milton.'" *PMLA*, 51 (1940): 102–18.

———. *The Life Records of John Milton.* 5 vols. New Brunswick, NJ: Rutgers University Press, 1949–58.

Hanford, James Holly. "The Rosenbach Milton Documents." *PMLA*, 38 (1923): 290–96.

Hart, D. Bentley. "Matter, Monism, and Narrative." *Milton Quarterly*, 30 (1996): 16–26.

Henry, Nathaniel. "John Milton, Anglican." *Renaissance Papers* (1969): 57–66.

Hill, Christopher. *Milton and the English Revolution*. New York: Viking, 1978.

———. "Professor William B. Hunter, Bishop Burgess, and John Milton." *Studies in English Literature*, 33 (1993): 165–93.

Hunter, William B. "Herbert and Milton." *South Central Review*, 1 (1984): 22–37.

———. "Milton on the Passions." *Milton Studies*, 25 (1989): 213–43.

———. *The Descent of Urania*. Lewisburg, PA: Bucknell University Press, 1989. Includes reprints of "The Power of Matter" (1952), "Milton and the Waldensians" (1971), "The Theological Context of the Christian Doctrine" (1976), "The Double Set of Temptations in *Paradise Regained*" (1980), and, with Stevie Davies, "Milton's Urania" (1988).

———. "The Provenance of the *Christian Doctrine*." *Studies in English Literature*, 32 (1992): 129–42, 163–66.

———. "The Provenance of the *Christian Doctrine*: Addenda from the Bishop of Salisbury." *Studies in English Literature*, 33 (1993): 191–207.

———. "Animadversions upon the Remonstrants' Defenses against Burgess and Hunter." *Studies in English Literature*, 34 (1994): 195–203.

———. "Ramblings in Elucidation of the Authorship of the *Christian Doctrine*." See McColgan, 41–50.

Hunter, W.B., C.A. Patrides, and J.H. Adamson.

Works Cited

Bright Essence: Studies in Milton's Christology. Salt Lake City: University of Utah Press, 1971. Includes reprints of Hunter, "The Meaning of 'Holy Light,'" (1959), "Milton on the Incarnation," (1960), "Milton's Muse," (1964), "The War in Heaven: The Exaltation of the Son" (1969), and Adamson, "Milton and the Creation" (1962).

Kelley, Maurice. "Milton's Debt to Wolleb's *Compendium Theologiae Christianae.*" *PMLA*, 50 (1935): 156–65.

———. *This Great Argument. A Study of Milton's De Doctrina Christiana as a Gloss upon Paradise Lost.* Princeton, NJ: Princeton University Press, 1941.

———. "A Reply to William B. Hunter." *Studies in English Literature*, 34 (1994): 153–63.

Kerrigan, William. *The Sacred Complex.* Cambridge, MA: Harvard University Press, 1983.

Lewalski, Barbara. *Milton's Brief Epic.* Providence, RI: Brown University Press, 1966.

———. "Forum." *Studies in English Literature*, 32 (1992): 143–54.

Lieb, Michael. *The Dialectics of Creation.* Amherst, MA: University of Massachusetts Press, 1970.

———. "Milton and the Anthropopathetic Tradition." *Milton Studies*, 25 (1989): 213–43.

———. *Milton and the Culture of Violence.* Ithaca, NY: Cornell University Press, 1994.

MacCallum, H.R. "Milton and Figurative Interpretation." *University of Toronto Quarterly*, 31 (1962): 397–415.

Madsden, William G. *From Shadowy Types to Truth.* New Haven: Yale University Press, 1968.

Martin, Catherine Gianelli. "'Pregnant Causes Mixt':

The Wages of Sin and the Laws of Entropy in Milton's Chaos." See McColgan, 161–82.

Masson, David. *The Life of John Milton.* 6 vols. London, 1877–96.

McColgan, Kristin Pruitt, and Charles W. Durham, eds. *Arenas of Conflict: Milton and the Unfettered Mind.* Selinsgrove, PA: Susquehanna University Press, 1997.

Miller. Leo. "Milton's State Letters: The Lünig Version." *Notes and Queries,* 17 (1970): 412–14.

———. *John Milton's Writings in the Anglo-Dutch Negotiations, 1651–1654.* Pittsburgh: Duquesne University Press, 1992.

Milton, John. *The Works of John Milton.* 18 vols. New York: Columbia University Press, 1931–38.

———. *Complete Prose Works of John Milton.* 8 vols. New Haven: Yale University Press, 1954–82.

———. *The Complete Poetry of John Milton,* ed. John Shawcross. New York: Doubleday-Anchor, 1971.

New Testament. *Novum Domini Noster Jesu Christi Testamentum* Syriacé. *Cum Versione Latina,* ed. Martin Trost. Anhalt, Germany, 1621.

Norton, Mary F. "'The Rising World of Waters Dark and Deep': Chaos Theory and *Paradise Lost.*" See McColgan, 140–60.

Ogden, James. "Bishop Burgess and John Milton." *Bibliographical and Contextual Studies,* Nos. 29 and 30. Lampeter, Wales: The Founders' Library, University of Wales, 1997, 79–98.

Parker, William R. *Milton: A Biography.* 2 vols. Oxford: Oxford University Press, 1968.

Pecheux, Sister M. Christopher. *Milton: A Topographical Guide.* Washington, DC: University Press of America, 1981.

Works Cited

Pepys, Samuel. *Letters and the Second Diary*, ed. R.G. Howorth. London: J.M. Dent, 1932.

Pittion, J.P. "Milton, La Place, and Socinianism." *Review of English Studies*, 23 (1973): 138–46.

Polanus, Amandus. *Enchiridii Locorum Communium Theologicorum*. Basel, 1600.

———. *The Substance of Christian Religion*. London, 1608.

Read, Allen Walker. "The Disinterment of Milton's Remains." *PMLA*, 45 (1930): 1050–58.

Rumrich, John. "Milton's God and the Matter of Chaos." *PMLA*, 110 (1995): 1035–46.

———. *Milton Unbound*. Cambridge, U.K.: Cambridge University Press, 1996.

Schaff, Phillip. *The Creeds of Christendom*. 3 vols. New York: Harper, 1931.

Scherpbier, Herman. *Milton in Holland*. Amsterdam, 1923.

Schoenbaum, Samuel. *William Shakespeare: A Documentary Life*. New York: Oxford University Press, 1975.

Schwartz, Regina. *Remembering and Creating: Biblical Creation in "Paradise Lost."* Cambridge, U.K.: Cambridge University Press, 1993.

Scott-Craig, Thomas S.K. "The Craftsmanship and Theological Significance of Milton's *Art of Logic*." *Huntington Library Quarterly*, 17 (1953): 1–16.

Selden, John. *John Selden on Jewish Marriage Laws*, trans. Jonathan R. Ziskind. Leiden: E.J. Brill, 1991.

Sellin, Paul. "John Milton's *Paradise Lost* and *De Doctrina Christiana* on Predestination." *Milton Studies*, 34 (1996): 45–60.

———. "The Reference to John Milton's *Tetrachordon*

in *De Doctrina Christiana.*" *Studies in English Literature*, 37 (1997): 137–49.

Sewell, Arthur. *A Study in Milton's Christian Doctrine.* London: Oxford University Press, 1939.

Shawcross, John. *Milton: The Critical Heritage.* New York: Barnes and Noble, 1970.

———. *Milton, 1732–1801: The Critical Heritage.* London: Routledge and Kegan Paul. 1972.

———. "A Survey of Milton's Prose Works." *Achievements of the Left Hand*, eds. Michael Lieb and John Shawcross. Amherst, MA: University of Massachusetts Press, 1974.

———. "Amanuenses" and "Attributions" in *A Milton Encyclopedia*, ed. William B. Hunter, et al. 9 vols. Lewisburg, PA: Bucknell University Press, 1978–83.

———. *Milton: A Bibliography for the Years 1624–1700.* Binghampton, NY: Medieval and Renaissance Text Society, 1984.

———. "Forum." *Studies in English Literature*, 32 (1992), 155–62.

Sotheby, Samuel Leigh. *Ramblings in the Elucidation of the Autographs of Milton.* London, 1861.

Sprunger, Keith L. *The Learned Dr. William Ames.* Urbana, IL: University of Illinois Press, 1972.

Stanwood, Paul. "Of Prelacy and Polity in Milton and Hooker." *Heirs of Fame: Milton and Writers of the English Renaissance*, eds. Margo Swiss and David A. Kent. Lewisburg, PA: Bucknell University Press, 1995.

Swanson, Reuben J. *New Testament Greek Manuscripts. Variant Readings. Matthew.* Sheffield, U.K.: Sheffield Academic Press, and Pasadena, CA: William Carey International University Press, no date.

Works Cited

Todd, H.J. *Some Account of the Life and Writings of John Milton*. London, 1826.
Turner, W. Arthur. "Milton's Aid to the Polyglot Bible." *Modern Language Notes*, 64 (1949): 345.
van Stam, F.P. *The Controversy over the Theology of Saumur, 1635–1650*. Amsterdam and Maarssen: APA-Holland University Press, 1988.
Voetius, Gisbertus. *Politicae Ecclesiasticae*. Amsterdam, 1666.
West, Robert H. *Milton on the Angels*. Athens, GA: University of Georgia Press, 1955.
Westminster Confession of Faith. See Schaff.
Wolleb or Wollebius. See Beardslee.
Woodhouse, A.S.P. "Notes on Milton's Views on the Creation: The Initial Phase." *Philological Quarterly*, 28 (1949): 211–36.

Index

Adamson, Jack, 121, 171, n. 10
Allsup, James O., 11
Ames (Amesius), William, 25, 27, 29, 31, 73–75, 82, 83, 105
Amyraut, Moyse, 85
Angels, time of creation of, 126–27; diet and sex of, 133–34
Anglican Church; see Church of England
Anonymous Biographer; see Skinner, Cyriack
Areopagitica, 93
Arianism, 54, 100–4, 116; see also Son of God
Armstrong, Brian G., 169, nn. 13, 14, 15
Artis Logicae (*Art of Logic*), 115–16, 122, 148, 153; see also Ramist logic
Attributions to Milton, 4
Aubrey, John, 13, 19–20, 26, 36
Augustine, St., 122, 126–27

Beal, Peter, 163, n. 2
beget, twofold meaning of, 111–12
blasphemy, 93
Book of Common Prayer; see Church of England
Brown, Cedric, 136

Burgess, Thomas, Bishop of Salisbury, 4–7, 46, 51–52, 71, 101–2
Burton, Robert, 129–31

Cameron, John, 77
Campbell, Gordon, 11, 47–48, 153, 161, n. 6; 164, n. 3; 165, nn. 6, 10, 13; 166, n. 27; 167, n. 8; 175, nn. 8, 12
Cappel (Capell), Louis, 82, 84–85, 105
Carey, John, 9
Catholicism, Roman, 51, 52, 93–95
chaos, 2, 121–26
Church of England, 14–16, 71–72, 81, 100, 104, 157; see also St. Giles Church at Cripplegate
Collier, John Payne, 47, 48
Commonplace Book, Milton's, 2, 82
Correspondence, Milton's, 86
Courcelles, Étienne, 76, 78, 86
creation *ex deo*, 1, 100, 121–23, 131
creation of heaven and the angels, 126–27
Curry, Walter C., 175, n. 1

Danielson, Dennis, 175, n. 1

Index

Defenses, Milton's, 46, 135–36, 147, 154–56, 174, n. 7
divorce, 23–24, 137–47
Doctrine and Discipline of Divorce, 31, 81, 82, 139
Dort, Synod of, 72
Durham, Charles, 10

Elton, William, 37
Epistolarum Familiarium, 42–43
essence, definition of, 115–16

Fallon, Robert T., 11, 43, 172, n. 13
Felbinger, Jeremias, 76
Fixler, Michael, 175, n. 1
French, J. Milton, 41, 162, n. 4; 163, n. 10; 165, 18, 21

Hanford, James Holly, 36, 37
Hart, D. Bentley, 173, n. 9
hell, 2
Henry, Nathaniel, 160, n. 6
heresy, definition of, 93–96
Hill, Christopher, 10, 14, 51–55, 89, 170, n. 9
Hooker, Richard, 72–73

incarnation, dogma of the, 117–18
Index Theologicus, Milton's, 2
invocation of God, Milton's, 107–8, 136

Kelley, Maurice, 9, 10, 27, 38–39, 49–51, 55–56
Kerrigan, William, 171, n. 10

Lampeter Library, St. David's College (Wales), 6, 7
law, authority of Old Testament, 65–70
Lemon, Robert, 5, 18, 36, 47, 48
Lewalski, Barbara, 4, 10, 60, 87, 99, 110, 113, 114, 137, 161, n. 3; 175, n. 1
Lieb, Michael, 123, 161, n. 3; 175, n. 1
Limborch, Philip van, 17
Literae Pseudo-Senatûs, 17, 43
logic; see Ramist logic
Low, Anthony, 11, 166–67, n. 1

MacCallum, H.R., 112
manuscripts, Milton's, 16–18
Martin, Catherine G., 173, n. 5
Masson, David, 41, 136
matter, power of, 132
McColgan, Kristin P., 10
Melchizedek as model for tithing, 60–61, 91
metaphor, employment of, 112–13
Miller, Leo, 165, n. 8; 166, n. 24
monism; see creation *ex deo*

190

Index

mortalism, 51
Moslem allusions, 57–58

Norton, Mary F., 173, n. 5

Of Education, 163, n. 5
Ogden, James, 6
Ong, Walter, 115

"Packer, Mr.," 32, 37, 39, 152
Paradise Lost, 15, 50, 51, 58, 61, 67–68, 107–14, 116, 117, 122–31, 133–34, 136
Paradise Regained, 15, 116–17
Parker, William R., 21, 41, 164, n. 5; 165, n. 14
Patten, Robert, 10
Picard, Jeremie, 22, 32, 35–40
Pitt, Moses, 43, 46, 48
Pittion, J.P., 84
Placaeus (la Place, Joshué), 82–4
Polanus, Amandus, 3, 82, 105
polygamy, arguments for, 142–44
private school, Milton's, 21, 25–31
Prynne, William, 73, 90, 91
Public Record Office, 5, 18, 35
Puritanism, 14, 15

Quakers, 65

Ralegh, Sir Walter's *Cabinet Council*, 3, 147
Ramist logic, 88, 115, 148, 153; see also *Artis Logicae*
Read, Allen Walker, 161, n. 3
Readie and Easie Way, 96, 108
Reason of Church Government, 73, 81
Richardson, Jonathan, 19
Rivet, Andrew, 86
Royal Society of Literature, 5, 7
Rumrich, John, 2, 166, n. 1; 173, n. 5

St. David's College, Lampeter, Wales, 6
St. Giles Church at Cripplegate, 13, 157
Saumur (France), 82–86
"Scale of Nature", 122, 128–33
Scherpbier, Herman, 163, n. 15
Schoenbaum, Samuel, 167, n. 8
Schwartz, Regina, 123
Scott-Craig, Thomas S.K., 173, n. 18
scripture, its authority, 63–65
Selden, John, 23–24, 46, 81, 138–39
Sellin, Paul, 11, 30, 74, 168, n. 9; 170, n. 1; 174, n. 6
Sewell, Arthur, 1, 8

Index

Shawcross, John, 4, 10, 11, 37, 44, 140, 144, 172, n. 14; 174, n. 7
Skinner, Cyriack, 18, 19, 20–25, 37, 139
Skinner, Daniel, 16–17, 23, 25, 33, 35–36, 40–48
Son of God, 1, 99–119
Sotheby, Samuel L., 37
Spelman, Henry, 91
Spirit, Holy, its authority; see scripture, its authority
Springer, Keith, 165, n. 6
Stanwood, Paul, 10, 72–73
State Papers, Milton's, 17, 18, 41–43
Stavely, Keith, 102
stylometric analysis; see Campbell, Gordon
subordinationism, 110
Sumner, Charles, 5, 7, 36, 166, n. 26
Swanson, Reuben J., 168, n. 9

Tetrachordon, 77, 82, 138–40
tithing, 57, 58, 61–62
Toland, John, 19
Tout, T.F., 6, 51
Turner, W. Arthur, 168, n. 7

Urania, 108

van Stam, F.P., 169, nn. 15, 16
Voetius, Gisbertus, 74–75

Waldensians, 59, 61, 170, n. 10
Walton, Brian, 53, 75–77
West, Robert H., 174, n. 12
Westminster Confession of Faith, 67, 72, 90, 105
Wharton, David, 11
will, Milton's, 16
Wolleb (Wollebius), John, 24, 25, 26–30, 82, 83, 87, 90, 105, 146
Wood, Anthony à, 19
Woodhouse, A.S.P., 123

**GENERAL THEOLOGICAL SEMINARY
NEW YORK**

	DATE DUE		

HIGHSMITH #45230 — Printed in USA